Riding the Canyons

by
Julie Davis Kooch

> Freda,
> I hope you come to understand why I love the canyon so much!
> Julie

Book design: Billie Judy
Cover design: Jonathan T. Stratman
Publisher: Ivy Gate Communications
Front cover photo: Sharon Gibson.
"Imnaha Canyon from a point near Tully Creek"

©Julie Davis Kooch 2016
Enterprise, Oregon 97828
chicojulie@gmail.com
541-426-3490

All rights reserved

ISBN-13: 978-1535307987
ISBN-10: 1535307986

DEDICATION

From the time I was a child I have had a passion for "canyon cowboying." As is told in my first book, *My Life on Joseph Creek*, I have been involved with canyon cattle ranching, in one form or another, all of my life. When Lee had to leave the Monument Ranch for health reasons in 1995, the canyon life was ripped from me once again!

I dedicate this book to Tom Birkmaier and Dwayne Voss, the ranchers who took me on as a day rider. I hate to even imagine what my life would have been like the last fourteen years without the opportunity to ride for these guys!

Tom Birkmaier was the first to take me on. I have never seen anyone who knows his range and cattle as thoroughly as Tom does. It became a joke among us, when I first started riding for Tom, that if we weren't sure where we were, all we had to do was radio Tom and say, "I am under this big pine tree." Tom would think for a minute then say, "I know exactly where you are. If you go..." And he *did* know where we were! Of course, there are thousands of big pine trees out there! If we lost some cattle, all Tom asked was that we tell him which direction they went so he would know where to go looking for them. I so appreciated his patience.

Dwayne Voss was the second rancher to hire me as a day rider. The first couple of times I rode for him, he pretty much kept me on the benches and "easier" terrain, but when I had ridden for him a few times, I guess I kind of proved myself, because he started sending me into steeper, more rugged places. Oh, the beauty I saw!

In that rugged country, sometimes the cattle "won." When it got to the place it was obvious that we were not going to "get it done" Dwayne would just say, "We'll come back tomorrow and pick up the pieces. They will probably have themselves pretty much straightened out by then." And usually they did—those old cows were smart!

I told Dwayne how much I appreciated the fact that when everything went wrong, he stayed cool! Two of his most common comments were, "If you're going to be in this business, sometimes things are bound to go sidewise." Another was, "Shoot Julie, if it was easy, we'd just have a bunch of kids out here." He was a pleasure to work for and with!

I say a big heartfelt THANKS to both of you guys. My life is fuller because of you!

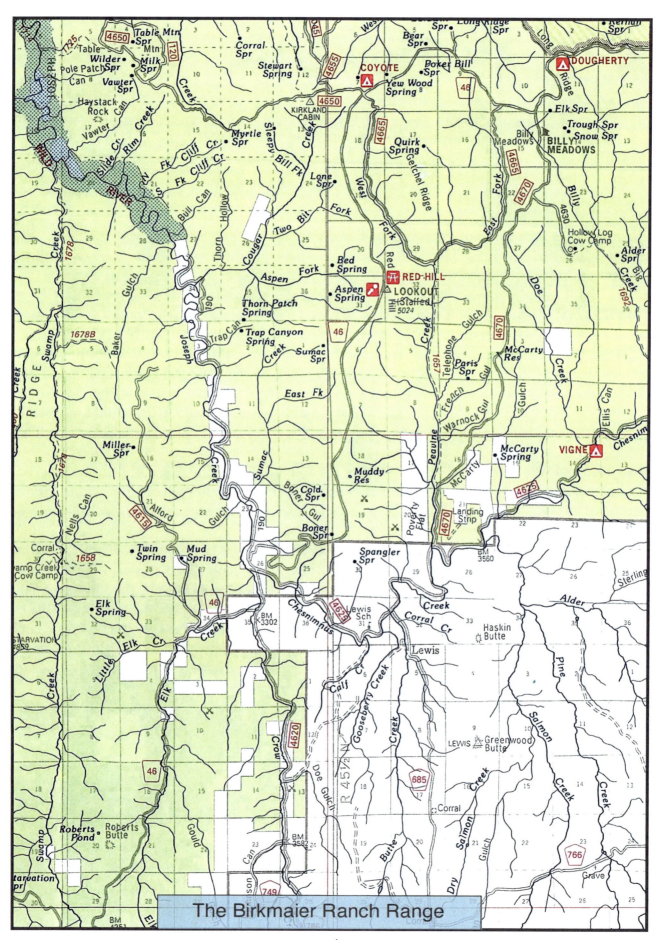

The Birkmaier Ranch Range

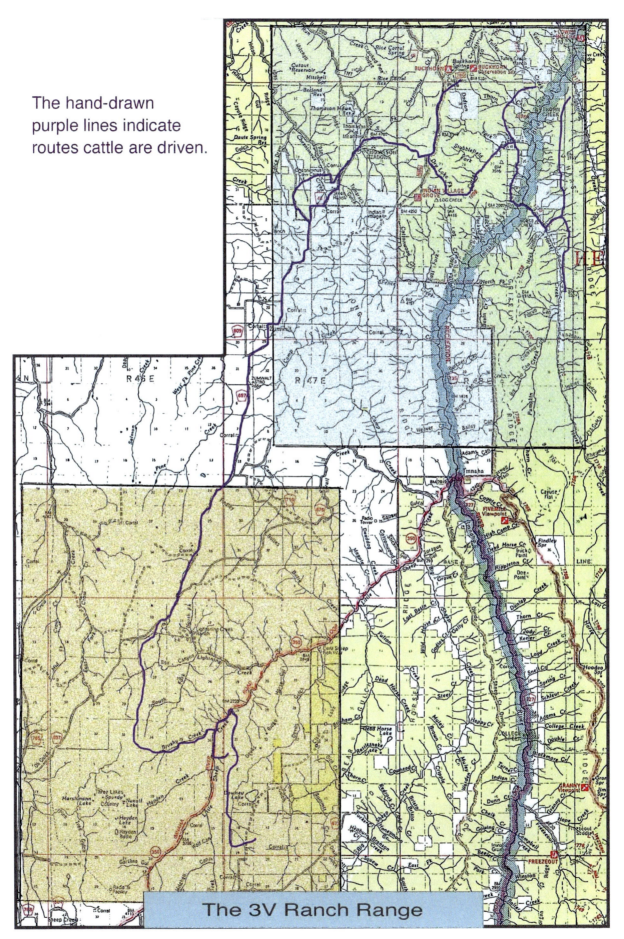

The hand-drawn purple lines indicate routes cattle are driven.

The 3V Ranch Range

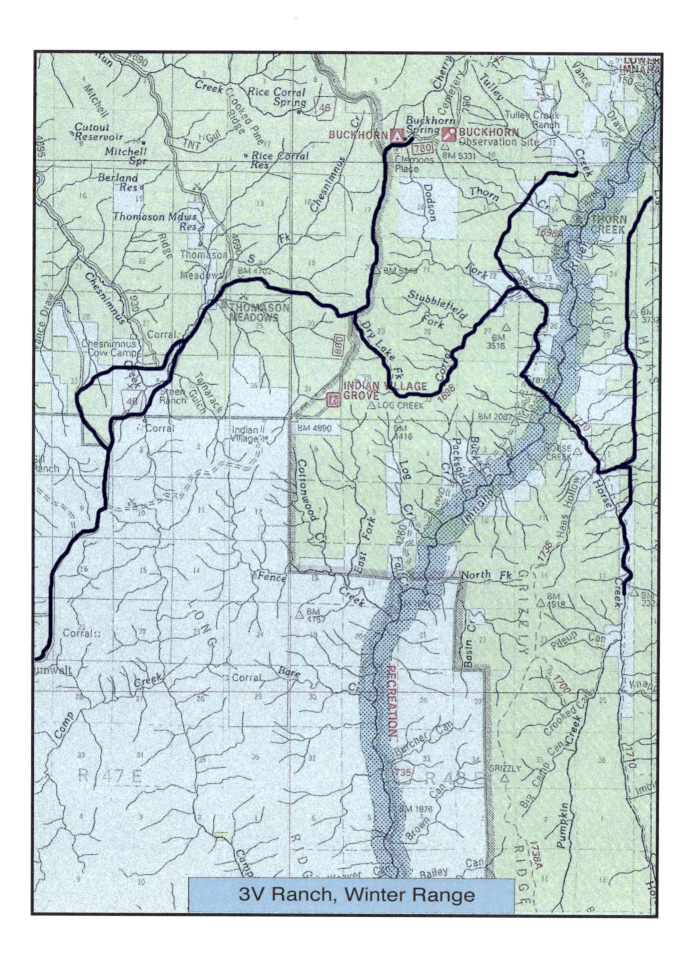
3V Ranch, Winter Range

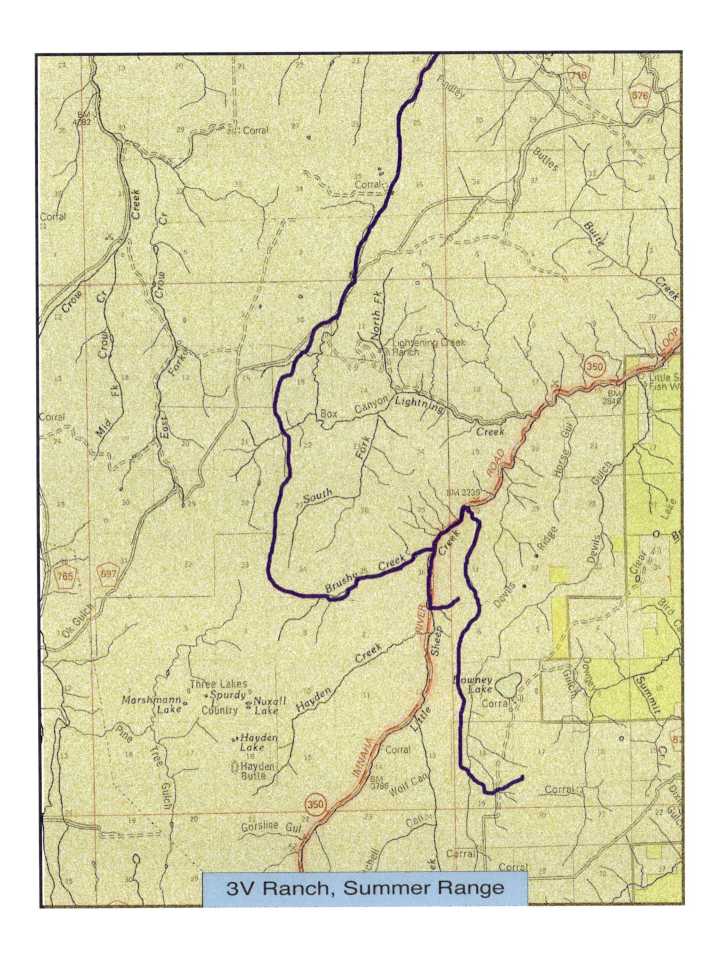

CONTENTS

Dedication iii
Map: Birkmaier Ranch Range. iv
Map: The 3V Ranch Range v
Map: The 3V Ranch Winter Range. vi
Map: The 3V Ranch Summer Range vii
Introduction ix

PART ONE — In the Meantime, In-Between Time
    Pig Operation 1
    Horses and Mules 5
        Doc 5
        Dick and Rocky 6
        Cindy and Mamie 8
        Sonny. 11
        Chip 16
        Mattie and Lucie 18
        Ozzie 23
    Wagon Trains. 25
    Pack Trips 32
    Trail Rides 43
        Asotin to Joseph 43
        Day Rides 47
    Marr Flat Cattle Company 50

PART TWO — Riding for the Birkmaier Ranch
    Getting Started. 53
    The Hearing Place 58
    The Swamp Creek Range 63
    The Cougar Creek Range 68
    Bulls 77

PART THREE — Riding for the 3V Ranch
    The Call 82
    Spring of 2013 92
    The Freeze of 2013-2014 110
    Fall and Winter of 2014-2015 115
    Spring Gather and Moving Cattle 2015 . . . 126
    Fall and Winter of 2015-2016 140
    Spring of 2016. 163
Conclusion 182

Acknowledgements 183

INTRODUCTION

A few years after my book, *My Life on Joseph Creek* was published, people started asking me when I was going to write another book. My emphatic reply was that I had only one book in me, the story of my life, and it had already been written! People kept persisting, and I did keep having more and more exciting experiences, thus I found myself softening to the idea. As I would share some exciting adventure, they would say, "See, there is another story!" Thus this book was conceived.

As told in *My Life on Joseph Creek*, there were several occasions, because of various circumstances, the 'canyon life' was ripped from me. It broke my heart, but I didn't just roll over and die! In the meantime, I went on with life in spite of a 'hole' in my heart. When opportunities allowed me back into the canyons, it was not full time, so in between times of being able to follow my greatest passion—"canyon cowboying"—I have done wonderful, exciting things! Thus the title of Part One: 'In the Meantime, In Between Time.'

I started riding for Tom Birkmaier of the Birkmaier Ranch in the fall of 2003, and continue to ride for him to the present. In the spring of 2013 I started riding for Dwayne Voss on the 3V Ranch, and I continue to ride for him also.

Some of the people and places in this book were also mentioned in my first book, *My Life on Joseph Creek*. You will better understand the significance of some places identified in pictures if you have read that one first. Some of the stories in this book happened in the same time frame as *My Life on Joseph Creek*; they simply were not included in that book.

Rather than telling the stories in chronological order I've clustered them topically. That is, I put the stories of riding for the Birkmaier Ranch in one section and the stories of riding for the 3V Ranch in another. I've included dates of most stories to help the reader understand the timing of the events.

I have always been told that horses are equalizers, and the older I get the more I realize how true it is. I've been riding the canyons all my life, but now I'm riding steeper, more rugged country than I was riding when I was forty years old! God has blessed me with excellent health, so when someone says that "seventy is the new fifty," I agree, and am going to cling to that theory until it is proven wrong!

Over 400 photos show you where I rode and what I saw! Except for the ones I'm in, of course, I photographed most of the pictures. The few I didn't take, I credited to their respective photographers.

As in *My Life on Joseph Creek*, the language of the canyon cowboys is "spoken here," so relax and enjoy!

PART ONE
IN THE MEANTIME ... IN BETWEEN TIME

Pig Operation

I developed quite a pig-raising operation after my kids graduated from high school in 1987. They had pig projects in 4-H and FFA. When they left for college I bought their sows. I started with four or five, but as the years passed and the operation grew, I ended up with twenty-three sows.

Katrina feeding a bummer piglet.

Each sow had her own pen and I fed them all by hand—there was no automation. I was it! I drug a hose to each pen to water them and wet down the feed. The problem with feeding them dry grain was that the grain would ball up on the rings in their nose, to the extent that it would actually restrict their breathing. When it was cold I would water them in the morning before I went to school so they would have a chance to drink before the water froze.

Each sow had her own pen.

When the sows were dry—not nursing babies—I turned them out on pasture and they grazed like cattle. If I didn't keep them rung—rings in their noses—they would tear up the ground by rooting. Everywhere they tore up the ground, it turned into a thistle and weed patch.

Sows ran loose in the pasture.

Pigs are different from cows in that the breeding cycle can be easily controlled. When a litter of pigs is weaned or taken from the sow, the sow then came into heat on the third day and bred on the fifth day.

I had a farrowing room with only six farrowing crates so it was necessary that not all of the sows farrow (give birth) at the same time. To prevent this, I weaned three or four litters, then waited several days, maybe a week, then weaned several more litters.

Some boars weighed 800 lbs.

I kept records on all of the sows. Some consistently farrowed 128 days after the previous litter had been weaned, some 132 days, and some would vary from 126 to 135 days, and so forth. The sows that farrowed on a consistent schedule made it easy for me to know when to get them in the crates. I didn't want to put them in too soon, because I tried to have them in the crates for as short a time as possible. When the piglets were a few days old and still on the farrowing crates, I docked the tails of all the piglets and castrated the male piglets. I caught the babies and put them in a box. After I docked their tails, castrated, and vaccinated them, I put them back in with their mama.

Simon slept with piglets under heat lamps

When castrating them, I held them upside down between my knees. Of course the minute I touched them, they squealed to high heaven, which really upset the sow. That's why it's so important to castrate and give shots while the sow is confined in the crate, otherwise she would have "gotten me!"

I had learned earlier that it was much easier to do all of this while the piglets were really small, when I could do it by myself. Earlier in my life I had to be the one to hold thirty to forty pound, or bigger pigs as they were being castrated, and it was no fun!

When I first started my pig operation I made the mistake of waiting until the pigs were too big, then I asked a friend of mine, Marilynn Davis, to come and hold them for me. She was a really good sport about it, but learned, in a hurry, to keep her mouth shut during the operation! I could see it would be a real test of friendship to ask anyone to do this on a regular basis. That's why I started castrating when they were only a few days old and I could do it by myself.

I had the sows farrow right after spring vacation at school, so I would be free over vacation. I was teaching school during the time of my pig operation. I had them farrow again in September after I got home from participating in the Pendleton Round-Up celebration.

I was very busy during farrowing time. I would be up by no later than 5:00 a.m. to get the pigs taken care of before going to school. I came home from school, fed the pigs, and cleaned farrowing crates until 9:00 or 10:00 at night.

My sows were not mean.

I kept a radio playing in the farrowing room to soothe the sows; it seemed to calm them. I can remember being on my hands and knees cleaning a farrowing crate one night when on the radio one of our local doctors was being interviewed. He was whining about how hard he had to work, as a rural doctor. He said it was like holding down two jobs. Needless to say, that didn't set very well with me! At least he was making good money—a lot more than I made at my "second job!"

Sharing a bed

When I had only a few sows, I fattened out the pigs, feeding them until they were ready for slaughter, about 250 pounds. I chopped all of my own grain with an old hammer mill that a friend found for me down in the Willamette Valley.

Randy Burns, from down around Lostine, was also raising hogs at that time. He was so good to let me put my pigs on his truck when he took them to market. All I had to do was load them and haul them to Lostine and put them on his truck; he took it from there.

Feeder pigs about big enough to sell.

As I increased the number of sows, it got to be more than I could do to chop grain to fatten out that many pigs, so I started selling them as "feeders" at about 70 pounds.

At first I took them over to the sale yard in Lewiston, Idaho. Then somehow I got hooked up with a guy out by Oakesdale, Washington, which is northeast of Colfax, Washington, up in the Palouse country. He always gave me a good price and paid me a dollar a head for delivering them.

I had a stock trailer, which I pulled with my '72 Scout II. There was no problem taking the pigs that were born in the spring, because they would be ready to ship in late spring or early summer. It was a different story for the pigs born in September and October. They had to be delivered in December through January.

Between Enterprise and Lewiston was the Rattlesnake Grade, then from Lewiston I had to pull the grade up to the Palouse country. The Palouse country could be a windswept, icy area if you got caught in a blizzard! The Scout had an 8-cylinder engine and enough power to pull the grades, even when pulling the stock trailer full of pigs. I always carried a Handy-Man Jack and a few blocks, to block the wheels, and put under the tongue of the trailer, in case I ever had to unhook.

On one trip the receiver apparatus that the trailer hitch attached to under the Scout, broke loose and the weight of the pigs caused it to bend down until it was dragging on the pavement. I was between Colfax and Oakesdale, Washington when this happened. I was assessing the situation when a little old man came along and insisted that he hook onto the trailer and take it on to my destination. After we had hooked the trailer to his rig, we put a hydraulic jack under the bent piece of my hitch, and were able to bend it back up to where I could hook the trailer onto it after the pigs were unloaded. I followed the man on to the pig farm where we unloaded the pigs. We then hooked the trailer back onto the Scout. Without the pigs, the trailer was light enough on the hitch that I could pull it home.

A dear old gentleman, Wayne Clark, who lived on a place out north of Enterprise, and was a friend of mine, insisted that I use his Ford Ranger to take the next few loads of pigs. The Ford didn't have the power of the Scout so I had to just crawl up the grades and creep down the other side. I didn't want to "push it" because I was afraid of blowing up the engine. As I look back on it now, I am amazed that I didn't blow up the engine in that little rig in spite of my being so careful!

A friend, Lee, was able to get away from the ranch where he worked, and accompany me on one of the pig-delivering trips. It was one of the winter trips and the days were short, so it was dark when we loaded pigs in the morning and dark by the time we got back into the county that night.

We were at mile marker fourteen, which is between the Joseph Canyon View Point and the head of the Vawter trail when all of a sudden a man staggered onto the highway in front of us and was waving his arms frantically. It was cold so he was all bundled up, to the point we could not see who it was. It turned out to be Dave Nelson, who is the brother of my sister-in-law, Marlene Davis. Jim Birkmaier was also there. They were about frozen. I got in the little back seat of the rig so the guys could be up front next to the heater. As they thawed out they started telling us the story of what had happened that day.

Jim had a trap line down Joseph Creek and he needed to check it, so he had his dad, Bud Birkmaier, take him and Dave down Joseph Creek to the end of the road, to where the Monument Ranch house was located. The guys hiked down the Joseph Creek Trail, checking the traps as they went. Rather than hike all the way back up to the Monument Ranch house they climbed out of the canyon to the North Highway, Highway 3. They figured this was the shorter route, thus would probably save them time, which was important because the days were so short that time of year.

Bud was to come out the North Highway in late afternoon and pick them up. The guys had planned the route they would take to get out of the canyon so knew the location where they would reach the highway on top. The hike down the canyon took them longer than they had planned, but they made it fine. Down in the canyon bottom it was milder than on top, so there was no snow and the hiking was quite easy.

When the traps were all checked and the guys started climbing up the canyon wall they started getting into a little snow. Of course the higher they got, the deeper the snow became. The climbing got difficult, slowing them down and "burning a lot of daylight." When they were near the top, the snow depth increased drastically; out on top it was up to mid-thigh! They floundered through this snow, becoming colder and more exhausted with each step, reaching the highway just moments before we arrived. Jim was trying to get a fire started when Dave heard our rig and staggered onto the highway to stop us.

We knew Bud would be along the highway somewhere, looking for the guys, so as we proceeded toward Enterprise we slowed down with each approaching vehicle so we could see if it was Bud. Finally, when we were almost to the Double Arrow Vet Clinic we met yet another rig and it was Bud. Because we were pulling a trailer we couldn't turn around just anywhere. We went on to the Double Arrow Vet Clinic, turned around, and the race was on! Bud had gotten quite a head start on us so we didn't catch up with him for about six or eight miles. We started flashing our lights and got Bud's attention so he stopped.

Bud told us that he had been out to pick up the guys sometime earlier, and upon not being able to find them he had given up and gone back home, but he was worried about the them so turned around and headed back out, and that was when we met him.

The pig operation kept growing until the spring of 1999. That spring, the equipment for chopping grain, etc., started breaking down. I had to make a very important decision. If I chose to repair the equipment it would be quite expensive, which would then require me to continue the operation for another eight or ten years to recoup the expenses.

I decided I did not want to commit to another ten years of pigs, so I started the process of dispersing the operation. I did not breed the sows back when I weaned the piglets that spring, but instead I turned them out to pasture, fattened them up, and sold them. By the end of the summer I was "pigless." I felt "half retired!

HORSES AND MULES

Between 1995—when Lee got hurt and had to leave the Monument Ranch—and the present, there are seven "horse stories" that seem worthy of being told. I will tell the stories separately, though they overlapped on a timeline.

Here is a timeline to show the years I owned these animals.

Doc	1995-1997
Dick ad Rocky	1995-2004
Cindy and Mamie	1996-1999
Sonny	1997-2007
Chip	2003-????
Mattie and Lucie	2004-2013
Ozzie	2015-????

Doc
1995-1997

When Lee was hired on as the cow boss on the Monument Ranch, down Joseph Creek, the ranch was short of saddle horses so the boss told him to look for some horses. The boss, Dub Darnielle, knew that Lee would know better what he needed. Lee got a couple of horses from Carl and Caren Patten, one of which was Doc. He was the horse I rode the majority of the time when I was riding on the Monument Ranch. When we left the Monument Ranch I bought Doc. When it became apparent that Lee wouldn't be able to ride any more, I sold Doc to Ken and Carolyn Witty. He was one of those horses that you could put anybody on and they would be safe—he never spooked at anything! At the same time, you could get any "cowboying" done that needed done! He was a great horse. After Lee passed, I wanted to start riding again and was sorry I sold Doc. Ken and Carolyn let me borrow him quite often.

Clancy on Doc

Jessica on Doc, me on Chip

Caleb on Doc

Dick and Rocky
1995-2004

When Lee got hurt in September of 1995, he came to my place to heal up. When we left the Monument Ranch, Lee bought a saddle horse, Joker. I bought the team, Dick and Rocky, and also Doc, as mentioned previously. With Lee's injuries he could still drive the team, but it soon became apparent that he would never ride again. I really couldn't afford to feed horses that weren't going to be ridden. I didn't feel right in going riding while leaving Lee sitting at home so we sold both of the saddle horses and decided that we would concentrate on draft horse activities.

Lee and I in covered wagon with Dick and Rocky

I figured that I needed to do something with the team to earn some money to offset the feed costs. It was then that I developed "The Rising Sun Rides." I provided wagon rides for celebrations and special occasions.

We turned an old feed wagon of mine into an oversized covered wagon which could seat 20-25 people depending on their size. The wagon provided a very comfortable ride, protected from the sun and rain.

One ride I offered was a wagon ride/cowboy cookout combination. The day before the "cookout" I spent all day in food preparation. The morning of the ride, Lee and I went to the site of the "cook out" and set up the shelter and the tables. In the afternoon we loaded the people at Joseph, then Lee drove the horse drawn wagon to a little cabin, at the foot of the mountains, up Hurricane Creek. I went on ahead to finish the set-up and get the meat cooking.

Headed to the Cowboy Cookout

Rocky and Dick

Though this was a cowboy cookout in a rustic setting, it was done in style. The tables were spread with handkerchief print cloths, the food was served on white china plates, and the drink in stemmed goblets. Appetizers included, among other things, chocolate-drizzled fruit. There was a choice of steak or Cornish hen for the entrée, accompanied by cowboy beans, bread, a variety of salads, nonalcoholic beverages, and dessert. When it was time to load up and head back to Joseph, invariably the guests expressed a desire to stay longer; they were so relaxed and enjoying themselves so much. After Lee left with the guests, I packed up all of the uneaten food, dirty dishes, and utensils then packed them into my rig. I then carried all of the tables, chairs, and grills back into the cabin for storage. I took down the large circus-type "big top" which had no walls, rolled it up and carried/drug it into the cabin. I surveyed the area to find and remove any debris, which may have fallen to the ground.

Taking Mr. Rayburn to cemetery   Lee giving rides for Jessica's birthday   A family bobsled ride

I tried to keep the grounds in a manicured state. With the supplies stored in the cabin, the grounds cleaned, and all of the food supplies packed in my rig, it was finally time to head home.

While I was doing this, Lee drove the team and wagon back to Joseph where he unloaded the guests. He then unhitched the team, loaded them, and drove home to unharness the team and put them out to pasture.

Dick & Rocky, Cindy & Mamie 4-abreast team

I stored perishables in a refrigerator then put all of the table service, cooking and serving dishes, and utensils in a large basin to soak overnight. It was usually about midnight by the time I fell into bed. I would get up early Sunday morning and wash all of the dishes, trying to get it done in time to make it to church.

Dick and Rocky pulling my covered wagon

During this time Lee and I gave Christmas rides in Lostine. The Presbyterian Church hired us to come and give rides, as their gift to the community. The Enterprise Chamber of Commerce hired us to give rides in Enterprise, and also to help deliver Christmas packages. We carried the casket of an old gentleman from a church in La Grande to his final resting place in the La Grande cemetery. We also pulled in the Westward Ho Parade, which is part of the Pendleton Round-Up celebration. We gave rides for private parties and took fun rides with family and friends. We made a lot of memories.

Jessica's Girl Scout Troop on a bobsled ride

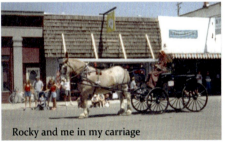

Rocky and me in my carriage

With Lee's passing in the spring of 1999 I no longer had a driver for the cookouts. I was worn out by the end of each weekend. I was tied down all the school year with my teaching, then spent all of my weekends all summer with these dinner rides. There was no time for trips into the high mountains. It wouldn't be the same with Lee gone—all of these thoughts kept replaying in my mind, which brought me to the decision to abandon the business and call it quits. We had had a fun few years, but there comes a time when it's time to move on.

Lynn Dohle, Katrina, and Clancy feeding Mr. Boucher's cows

Jessica driving Dick and Rocky

Me, attempting to plow with walking plow

Dick and Rocky in Westward Ho parade

I kept Dick and Rocky, even after Lee passed, and used them in many fun events as will be told in the stories to follow. I used them in plowing bees, pulled in parades, did weddings, and gave Christmas rides in Wallowa, Lostine, and Enterprise. I also participated in wagon trains sponsored by the Oregon Trail Interpretive Center at Baker City, Oregon, and wagon trains in the Blue Mountains, sponsored by the Pendleton Round-Up and Happy Canyon.

By 2004 I knew Dick and Rocky were getting old enough that if I was ever going to sell them, it had to be soon. My old friend, Gene Westberg, still enjoyed driving, but did not have a reliable team. He had a great old mare, but nothing trustworthy to drive with her. His family was afraid he was going to get hurt.

It was one of those win-win situations. I would sell the team at a price Gene could afford, thus they would have a good home for the remainder of their lives, and Gene would have a trustworthy team he could enjoy driving. After participating in the Pendleton Round-Up events in September 2004, I delivered the team to Gene who was living over around Baker at that time.

Cindy and Mamie
1996-1999

In 1996, Raymond (Cy) Kooch, my ex-husband's uncle, who live around Hermiston, Oregon, had a team of three-year-old Clydesdale mares for sale, Mamie and Cindy. Lee and I went to look at them. They were beautiful—black with all the white trimmings. They seemed to have good dispositions and I fell in love with them.

Cy had driven the mares five times in a round pen so they were just started; not even what you would call "green broke." Cy said Mamie might possibly be with foal, but he wasn't sure. I bought them and brought them home. The following spring Mamie did have a foal, Sonny. Lee and I worked with the mares all that winter, having them pull various wagons and a bobsled. I purchased a vis-à-vis carriage and a trailer large enough to haul the carriage and the team at the same time. I wanted to provide nice accommodations when doing weddings and special events. I had been using an older Surrey with a fringe on top. The mares did so well that we used them for weddings, parties, parades, and to pull in the Westward Ho Parade in Pendleton. Lee drove them and I drove Dick and Rocky.

Cindy and Mamie pulling vis-à-vis

In the spring of 1998, Gene Westberg, from around Baker City, Oregon sponsored a "plowing bee" on a ranch near Haines, Oregon. Lee and I took both the teams—Dick and Rocky, Cindy and Mamie. We enjoyed it so much we came home "with the bug."

Below is a clipping from the May 6, 1998 *The Observer*, of Lee driving Dick, Cindy and Rocky at the Double L Ranch horse-plowing event.

PLOWING, THE OLD-FASHIONED WAY

GENTLE GIANTS AT WORK: Lee Scott of Enterprise drove an old John Deere 560 plow Saturday morning in an old-fashioned horse-plowing event at the Double L Ranch at Wingville, northwest of Baker City. The trio of work horses — Dick, a Belgian; Cindy Lou, a Clydesdale; and Rocky, a Belgian — are owned by Julie Kooch of The Rising Sun Rides, also of Enterprise.

In late fall of 1998 Lee's condition worsened drastically and it became apparent that he would no longer be able to participate in driving the teams. It wasn't practical for me to keep both teams so I sold Mamie and Cindy, the vis-à-vis, and the trailer as a package.

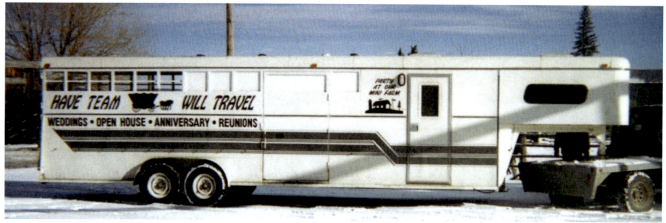
I sold Mamie and Cindy, the vis-à-vis, and the trailer as a package.

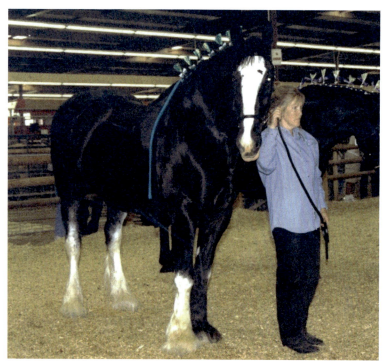
Mamie, after being rescued

I must admit that when the buyers came to take possession of "the package," I had a bad feeling. I could see that they did not know as much about driving as they had made me believe in our phone conversations. It appeared that the husband was buying the team for

Mamie, on a trail ride

his wife because she had developed some fantasy of becoming a "driver." The next part of Mamie and Cindy's story is just speculation on my part. My assumption is that something happened. The new owners had a "wreck" or something happened that scared them. This fear must have escalated to anger toward the mares, which developed into a lack of care, and I pray not—but maybe even abuse.

I first became aware of their situation several years after I had sold them, when a gal contacted me and said she had purchased Mamie at a sale. She said Mamie was thin and dirty. She had her head hanging out of the pen with a sad, pleading look in her eyes that seemed to say, "Please save me!" The gal said that at that moment she knew she just had to buy Mamie.

She took Mamie home, cleaned her up, and fed her adequately. Mamie blossomed into a beautiful mare. This gal took her to all kinds of horse shows where she won many ribbons and awards. She also rode Mamie on trail rides with friends.

Cindy had her own story. It seems that at that same sale she was bought by a vet from Montana for his daughter to ride. Things went fine for a while then Cindy developed a twisted gut. I am sure she received the best of care and that everything possible was done for her, but she had to be put down.

For years Larry Waters and Lee had dreamed of putting on a "plowing" here in Wallowa County. A "plowing" is an event at which people bring their teams and implements to work a field and prepare it for planting. It was finally going to happen the spring of 1999. People started arriving on Friday afternoon, coming from several counties. Lee never got to see that dream come true, as he passed away that Friday night.

Larry talked with Lee's brother Frank, who was the cow boss of a large ranch on the Imnaha at that time. Larry and Frank both agreed that Lee would want the plowing to go on, so it did. They worked the field Saturday and Sunday. It has ever since been called the Lee Scott Memorial Plow.

Understandably, I did not participate in that first plowing, but did for many years thereafter. I had the pleasure of driving all of my draft animals—horses and mules—at the plowings in the years that followed.

Me, discing at the Lee Scott Memorial Plow

Sonny
1997-2007

As I mentioned before, one of the Clydesdale mares, Mamie, did have a colt in the spring of 1997. I named him Sonny and he developed into one of the greatest horses I have had the honor of owning.

Immediately upon his birth I started "imprinting" sessions, which I continued several times a week for the first couple of weeks of his life. Imprinting is a technique where a person briskly rubs and pats the entire body of the colt; gently pokes fingers inside the ears, mouth, and nostrils, rubbing gently; some extremists of the practice even insert fingers into the rectum. Also the hoofs are tapped firmly with a stick or some other firm object.

The objective of this procedure is to make the animal more receptive to being handled as an adult animal. I, among many others, am convinced the procedure does make a difference in the way a horse responds when being trained later in life.

Mamie, with Sonny

Next I broke Sonny to lead. Then when he was a couple of months old I started saddling him with a child's saddle. At the same time, I started saddling Mamie and Cindy because I hoped to ride them later. I continued to work with Sonny, exposing him to as many experiences as possible. This continued until the spring of 1999 when he turned two years old. With Lee having passed away in April of that year I knew Sonny's training was going to be totally up to me. When I got ready to harness Sonny for the first time, Mark Porter came out to help me. Mark was a friend of Lee's and mine when we were on the Monument Ranch.

Sonny harrowing dry lots

Mark Porter helping me with Sonny

Sonny and Doc up the Wenaha

I "ground drove" Sonny in the round corral then started having him pull a railroad tie. Later I hooked him to a section of field harrow and moved out into a larger pen. At this time, I was also saddling him and riding him in the corral and a small pasture. Sonny was so tall I had to have a stool of some sort to get on him, so Mark rode him for me a few times.

On Memorial Day weekend of 2000, Ken and Carolyn Witty and I went on a pack trip up the Wenaha River from Troy, Oregon. Wanting to expose Sonny to as many different situations as possible I decided to pack him. He was so tall it was hard to get a pack up on him. I didn't put much weight on him, but he still sweat so profusely that it ran down his legs and dripped off his feet. We decided it had to be from nerves.

We turned the animals out in the meadow to graze in the mornings before we went on rides, then again in the evenings. When it was time to bring them in to be tied up, I would just step out into the edge of the meadow and call, "Sonny!" He would come galloping to me. Carolyn said, "My gosh, he's just like a dog!" As was typical of Sonny, he took everything right in stride, as though he had been in a pack string for years!

In the spring of 2000, when Sonny would turn three on June 20th, I knew it was time to get him out on the road and drive him in a team. A great teamster friend of mine, Larry Waters, agreed to come down and help.me. We hitched Sonny with Rocky, one of my Belgian geldings, and headed down the road. Sonny took to it like a duck to water. When we were finished driving that day, Larry was very complimentary about the job of groundwork I had done with Sonny. Larry then said, "Shoot, Julie, this horse is ready to go to town!" Coming from Larry, who is a great teamster, I considered it quite a compliment.

In August of that same year, Ken, Carolyn, and I packed my daughter, Katrina's in-laws into the Wallowa Mountains on a pack trip. Again we packed Sonny and he was a trooper. Paul Spriggs-Flanders was another friend of Lee's and mine. The first time I met him, he came out to help Lee and me get wood for some elderly friends, Wayne and Ival Clark. Paul didn't even know them, yet there he was—that was testimony of just what a good guy he was! Paul was about 6'4"—tall and lean. He could step up on Sonny as easily as I could a regular saddle horse. Sonny had been ridden only in the corral and a small pasture of mine. Paul agreed to ride Sonny on a few rides in the hills. We went into Davis Creek and on to Starvation Ridge, among other places. Sonny was one of those one-in-a-million-type horses. He did anything I asked of him. The problem was that I really didn't have much use for him, as I still had Dick and Rocky.

Sonny would work with any horse. Giving Blanche Maxwell a ride

I drove him at the plowings on the right, on the left, and in the middle of a "three-abreast" with Dick and Rocky. I used him occasionally at other events, but not nearly as much as he should have been used. I knew Sonny was being "wasted." Someone should have him that would use him more than I did, so I decided to sell him.

Dick, Sonny, and Rocky, three-abreast

Cousin Creighton Kooch, who had quite a herd of Clydesdale horses, and had driven six-up hitches for years, passed away. His wife Cheryl was dispersing the equipment and horses. It was really hard to sell a single draft horse. Most people wanted a team. I approached Cheryl to see if she had a horse I could match up with Sonny and sell them as a team. After some consideration Cheryl said she did have a horse I could team up with Sonny. She said he had been in a six-up a few times. His name was Max.

Paul on Sonny

When it came time to drive them, Tip Proctor came out to help me. Tip had driven mules and horses since he was a little boy. His dad had given him a span (team) of mules for his twelfth birthday. Tip had forgotten more about driving than most of us will ever know!

My neighbor, Mike Lathrop, who owns the pasture right across the road from my house, said I could drive my teams in his pasture. We hitched the team and proceeded to cross the road and enter the pasture. We had gone a little way into the pasture when Max bolted and tried to run.

Sonny didn't want to run so we just went in a circle. We got them lined out and Max bolted again. This behavior repeated itself several times then Max seemed to settle down somewhat, but Tip and I both knew he couldn't be trusted. We decided to call it a day while Max was doing somewhat better, and before he "tried something" again.

We left the pasture and got out in the road when Max blew up again. This time he reared and pawed at the air, sticking one front leg over the neck yoke. He then started jumping every which way and crowded Sonny into the barrow pit close to my front gate. Fortunately, a young man came by just then. He jumped out

Larry driving Sonny and Max

of his rig, grabbed Max's bridle, and with us pulling on the lines we were able to get him stopped. We discovered he had broken some straps on his harness. We unhitched the team from the wagon, led them to the barn, and unharnessed them. The harness would have to be repaired before we could drive again.

Tip had a bad shoulder and could not raise one arm above the shoulder, and had lost a lot of strength in the other arm. For the sake and safety of everyone, he felt it would be best if I found someone else to drive with me.

Once again I called on good ol' Larry—Larry Waters. Through the years Larry had come to my rescue many times. He had a lot of knowledge about driving and he was very stout. The day came when I was ready to drive again. The harness had been repaired. We harnessed the team, hitched up and drove across the road and out into the pasture. Because in the last wreck Max had gotten a front leg over the neck yoke, this time we tied his halter rope to the neck yoke, so if he reared, he would pull the neck yoke up too, thus he couldn't get a leg over it.

We drove for a while with Max messing around some, but not throwing any major fits. We were driving him on the left. All of a sudden he exploded! I don't remember everything he did, it all happened so fast, but when it was over he had swung to the left and was lying on the ground with his feet and legs extended under Sonny and his rear end was under the corner of the wagon.

Sonny and me   Photo by Gail Hillock

We could see that he wasn't hurt, though he occasionally gave a big groan. We considered several possibilities of what to do, one of which was to unhitch Sonny and get him away from there so if Max started thrashing and kicking he would not hurt Sonny, maybe even break his leg. We knew it would not be wise to have Max hitched to the wagon alone. If he got up and tried to run, there would be no stopping him without Sonny to hold him back. We decided to just let him lie there for a while.

Me, loving Sonny

He continued to occasionally raise his head, give out a loud groan then lay his head back down. We finally decided that I would get off the wagon and get ahold of Sonny's bridle/halter, then when Max raised his head I would pull Sonny to the right. Hopefully this would pull on Max's halter and he would scramble to his feet; that is exactly what happened! When Max was on his feet, he stood there, seeming somewhat dazed. We continued to drive for a while and Max never tried any more tricks. The nonsense was completely gone out of him!

We drove several more times with no problems, so we decided to move our driving sessions to the fairgrounds in Enterprise. There we drove around the racetrack and in the grassy area surrounded by the track.

Throughout the years Creighton and Cheryl had raised and sold many horses all around the country. There was a man in California, Neil Shepherd, who had bought their horses in years past. He was interested in buying another team. He was the great-nephew of Jack London, the author of Call of the Wild.

Neil and I—under Sonny's chin   Photo by Gail Hillock

Neil ran the Jack London Black Clydesdale Ranch, which was surrounded by the Jack London Park in California.

Cheryl contacted Neil and made arrangements for him to come and see the horses. I wanted Neil to see the horses "from start to finish" so I had not even caught them when he got to my place. I went out and called Sonny, and he came galloping to the barn with Max following him. Neil was impressed.

I told Neil that Sonny was well broke, but Max was still green—not completely broke. Neil helped catch and harness the team. One problem we hadn't completely resolved was that Max resisted taking the bit. Neil grabbed Max's bridle and headed for him as I headed for Sonny. Neil slipped the bit into Max's mouth as easily as slicing butter with a hot knife. That was the first thing Neil did that impressed me!

Cheryl hadn't been around during any of the driving sessions, but went to the fairgrounds when we took Neil to drive the team. We—Larry, Neil, Cheryl, and I—loaded up on the wagon, on which we had a partial load of straw. I took the lines, with Neil sitting next to me. I drove for a while showing Neil all the things the team would do.

When Larry and I had driven, I had done the majority of driving with Larry being there as my backup, thus the team was used to "the feel" of my driving. One day I had been very tired so I asked Larry to drive. The horses could feel the difference through the lines and started to mess around a little. After a little while Larry said, "Here take the lines, they can tell it is not you!" I took the lines back and Larry just smiled. That is just one of the things that I appreciated about Larry—he didn't have any ego problem. He had nothing to prove.

With this history, I was a little reluctant to hand the lines over to Neil, but after some time I knew it was time to do it. I handed over the lines and held my breath. The team never missed a beat! It was as though they never knew the lines had passed to someone new. Again Neil had impressed me!

A few years had passed after I sold Sonny to Neil. I was at a Small Farmers Journal Auction in Madras, Oregon. A tall good-looking man came up to me and said, "Julie?"

"Yes," I replied. "Do I know you?"

"I'm Neil Shepherd, the guy who bought Sonny."

"How did you know that it was me?"

"I recognized your voice."

I was amazed because Neil had been around me just a few hours several years ago, and now I had a cold and my voice was quite raspy. Again Neil amazed me! We had a long conversation about Sonny. Neil said that for as many times as he had hitched Sonny, Sonny had yet to make his first mistake. I was thrilled that Neil was so pleased with him.

I asked how Max was doing, to which Neil replied, "He's still green!" Neil then said, "By the way, I told my chore girl that if the horses are in the back of the pasture, all you have to do is call Sonny, and he will come on the run and the other horses will follow him!"

I did not have any further contact with Neil for several years then in the spring of 2015 I developed a strong urge to see Sonny once again. I called Neal and made arrangements to meet him at the park/ranch.

I invited three of my gal friends, Carolyn Witty, Carol Voss, and Gail Hillock to go with me to see Sonny. We made a road trip out of it, visiting places of interest along the way to the ranch/park, which is just out of Glen Ellen, California. Neil had taken the day off from work so he could show us around the place. He met us at the entrance to the park and guided us through the maze of roads that led to the barn and corrals where Sonny was kept.

When we arrived, Sonny had his head down in a feeder, eating hay. As I stepped out of the car I said, "Sonny," to which he jerked his head up, pointed his ears forward, and looked at me. Neil said, "He remembers you." And I am confident he did! I spent quite some time rubbing, petting, and patting him, and getting a lot of pictures.

Upon leaving I was flooded with conflicting emotions. It was kind of bittersweet. I was so happy that I had been able to see him once again, but at the same time kind of sad, knowing most likely this was the last time I would ever see him. He was eighteen at this time and most generally the big draft horses don't live beyond the early twenties.

Chip
2003-????

While I was having all of these great experiences with my draft animals there was a corner of my heart that was hollow. The fact was that I didn't have a saddle horse; I wasn't pushing cows in the canyons! I hadn't been without a saddle horse since I was a very small child. A part of me was missing. The canyons were calling me!

I started shopping for a saddle horse. Just any horse wouldn't do. I wanted a ranch-broke gelding, and not a "flatlander!" (A horse that had been ridden just on flat land.) I used several means of searching, one of which was "The Nickel." I searched regularly in this advertising paper then finally in September of 2003 a horse of interest showed up. He was a ranch gelding who had been ridden in the steep country on the breaks of the Snake River over by Richland/Halfway, Oregon.

I was very pleased with Chip.

I made a call, and a time was set up when I could go over and try him out. When visiting with the old man on the phone I had explained I wanted a horse that was well broken, but still young enough that I could get quite a few years out of him. The man said his horse was seven years old. When I arrived the old man had not caught him. He wasn't real easy to catch, but he was in a large pen with a bunch of horses that all acted like they would be hard to catch. I wanted the man to ride him and show me what he could do. Knowing I would be riding out in the timber where I would have to cross some logs that would be too big to step over, I wanted to see how he would jump them. There was a pile of lumber stacked in the barn lot. It was about three feet wide and two and one half feet high. When the guy rode "Toby" up to the pile and asked him to jump the pile, he did it very smoothly and without any hesitation. I was pleased.

Wilder and Vawter Flats as seen from Miller Ridge

Next we put my saddle on Toby and the old man saddled another horse and we went for a ride. We rode up a gravel road for a while then I decided I wanted to know what he would do when ridden away from another horse. I rode up through some brush and timber to where we were completely out of sight of the other horse. He did not resist the least bit. Again I was pleased. The price was right. I liked his looks—he had a good eye. He was a beautiful bay with a little white on three of his feet and a little white in his face. I didn't like the name "Toby" and I had decided when I started looking for a horse, I would probably name him "Chip" unless it just didn't fit. I paid for him, loaded him up and he became "Chip."

When I got him home I fed him some grain in a very small pen. I continued to do this for a few days so he became accustomed to coming into the pen, then when I wanted to catch him I just shut the gate and there was no place for him to go; he had to let me catch him. After some time, I used the same tactic, but just in a larger pen. He had become used to me by then and I was still able to catch him even in a bigger pen. I have always had the reputation of having more guts than brains. As I look back over the years I realize the reputation has been well earned! After I had Chip a few days I decided to take him to the canyons to see what he would do. I loaded up and trailered down Miller Ridge to an old log landing at the end of the road. I unloaded, mounted up, and headed down the ridge. In places, the trail went along the top on the narrow ridge; in others it went along the steep hillside, which was covered with thick, tall bunchgrass. These steep, grass-covered hillsides are great habitat for Chukars and Blue Grouse.

The grouse are notorious for waiting until you are right on them then flying up practically under your horse's belly.

I was on a steep hillside when we came upon some grouse. Thank goodness they flew up a few feet in front of us rather than under Chip's belly, but even at that they were so close that a lot of horses would have been spooked. Chip never spooked; he never even flinched. I was pleased and amazed, but realized it could have ended differently, and I started to realize that my plan for the day may not have been such a wise one. I can't remember having even told anyone where I was going that day. I proceeded on with my trip and was continuously impressed at how well Chip carried himself in that steep country.

The only flaw I found in him was that when he came to some brush, he wanted to back away from it rather than push through it. He was starting to get over that even by the end of that first ride. I went down Miller Ridge almost to Vawter Springs, dropped into the bottom of Swamp Creek and came back up it to Miller Canyon. I came up Miller Canyon to the top of Miller Ridge then back down Miller Ridge to my rig. My ride was completed without mishap and by the end of the day I realized how sure-footed and smart Chip was and how unwise I probably had been!

Later that fall I took Chip to the vet to get his shots, etc. As Vet Randy was working on Chip, he asked me how old Chip was. "You tell me," I said. Randy looked in Chip's mouth, examined his teeth then said he was certain Chip was five years old. He went on to show and tell me why he was so certain of this. It seems there are certain things that happen with the teeth of a horse when it is five.

This was a real switch! Usually the owner of a horse that is for sale, will tell you it is a couple of years younger than it really is, if he is not going to be honest with you. This guy had told me that Chip was a couple of years older than he really was! I figured the only reason for doing that was because I had said that I wanted a well-broke horse. The guy must have thought I would shy away from a five-year-old because I would feel he couldn't be as well broken as I wanted.

Chip has proved to be an exceptionally sure-footed horse and has enabled me to make many wonderful memories while riding him, as will be told in other stories in this book.

Mattie and Lucie
2004-2013

I had decided that whenever I got rid of Dick and Rocky I would replace them with a team of Belgian molly mules. Molly mules are female mules. I had told Larry and Juanita Waters to keep their ears and eyes open for such a team.

In 2004 I made a deal with Gene Westberg. I would sell him Dick and Rocky, but I wanted to keep them until the middle of September so I could pull in the Westward Ho Parade, which was part of the Pendleton Round-Up celebration. I would deliver them shortly after that.

The second weekend of September was always the Hells Canyon Mule Days. At this event, mules were shown at halter as well as in working classes. There also was a parade and a horse and mule sale. I used my covered wagon, pulled by Dick and Rocky, to haul the previous Grand Marshals in the parade and in the Grand Entry of the Saturday afternoon performance.

For Mule Days 2004, I had driven the team and wagon from my place to the fairgrounds, pulled in the parade, and was waiting to enter the Grand Entry when Juanita came dashing up to me to tell me that Tom Donavan had a team of mules that were just exactly what I had been looking for and they were for sale. He had them in a pen over by the track and some other people were looking at them.

Well, I couldn't just up and leave the team so I told Juanita there was no way I could go look at them right then. I had to pull in the Grand Entry, then unload my passengers and drive the team home, unharness them and put them out to pasture. I couldn't make it back until about 5:00 p.m. When I got back to the fairgrounds that evening, I went straight over to the mules. Tom was there so I asked if I could get in the pen and look them over. As I examined the mules I asked Tom all of the usual questions. I really liked what I saw and what Tom told me about them.

Mattie and Lucie pulling in Blue Mountain Wagon Train

Finally, I asked if anyone was ahead of me. He said there wasn't and whoever was first to say they wanted them, they would be the buyer. I bought them on the spot! I felt comfortable in doing this because in prior years, Lee had told me of this guy—Tom Donavan, over by Walla Walla, Washington—who was a horse and mule trader and he was as honest as the day was long. If Tom said it was thus and so, then that was exactly how it was! His reputation had preceded him. I told him that I didn't have my checkbook with me and I was going to grab a burger then go to the sale. Could I pick the mules up the next morning and pay for them then? Tom said that would be fine.

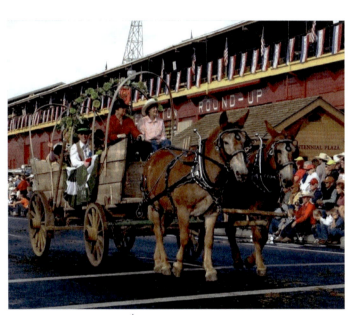
Pendleton Round-Up 100th Anniversary Westward Ho parade. Connie Worsech and me in front seat

When I went to pick them up the next morning this is the story Tom told me. I guess after I left the night before, the people from California came back to look at the mules again. They started quizzing Tom about the mules. After answering a few questions Tom told them that the mules were sold; a local gal had bought them. The couple was shocked, then angry. The man asked if I had actually paid for them. Tom told him that I was going to pay for them when I picked them up the next morning. The guy then asked Tom to let him write out a check, right then and there, for an amount greater than what Tom was asking. Tom told the guy, in no uncertain terms, that he, Tom, did not do business that way! As they walked away, the woman was really chewing on the guy's fanny for not buying the mules earlier that day.

Me, with Mattie and Lucie plowing

Tip Proctor driving Mattie and Lucie

Mattie and Lucie proved to be everything Tom had said they were, and more. I continued to participate in the wagon trains in the Blue Mountains with Carolyn riding shotgun. We did this for several years then Carolyn was unable to go for a couple of years, and I didn't want to go alone so I decided it was probably time to give it up.

I pulled in the Westward Ho Parade for quite a few years, carrying dignitaries of all kinds. I had different friends accompany me; one was Connie Worsech. She was with me in the parade the year the Pendleton Round-Up celebrated its 100th anniversary. It was quite a celebration. The parade set a record for the most horses in any one parade, ever. The parade was miles long. Fortunately, I was close to the beginning. When I was back to the staging area, there was still over a mile of horses lined up to go into the parade!

I used my mules, Mattie and Lucie, to plow at the Lee Scott Memorial Plow. One year there was a man with six miniature mules that he drove as a six-up. They were a handful and out of control a good share of the time. I had made several rounds around the field with my mules when this guy entered the field. From the start, his mules were pretty much out of control. All of a sudden they started to run. They went up the field a ways then circled back toward me. The guy would get them slowed down then they charged forward again.

I was out from the edge of the field and the fence by about seventy-five feet when the mules came charging toward me. I didn't know whether to pull over toward the fence and let them go by or stay where I was, leaving space for them to go between me and the fence. I decided to stay where I was so they could go on either side of me.

It ended up that they did not go on either side of me, but ran right up behind me with the lead pair surrounding me. I had the head of one of them over my right shoulder and the head of the other over my left shoulder. Their faces almost touched in my lap. The lines pulled tight and there was no place they could go, so they stopped. When I looked back and saw they were going to hit me, I hollered, "Whoa!" to my team. They stopped and just stood there through the whole ruckus! We were pretty close to where the spectators were, at the end of the field. I leaned off to the side so I could kind of see around my team and yelled, "We're going to need some help out here!" People had been watching the whole thing happen and several guys had started running out before I ever hollered.

There were enough guys that one got ahold of each mule and I was able to drive away from the mess. The mules had become tangled in their harnesses, breaking some of it, and some mules were even down. The guys got them untangled, led them back over to the trailer and tied them up.

I don't remember the guy driving them anymore that year. I know he didn't come back to the plowing for several years. I'm sure he was embarrassed. I do remember that when his mules hit me, and before the spectator guys could get out there to help us, I heard this guy say, "I am so sorry! I am so sorry!"

We both knew that if he had been driving a single team with a tongue between them, the tongue would have broken my back! I felt badly for him; I can still hear the fear in his voice! The fact is though, a person should never take any team that is not well broken to a place like that; you could cause yourself, someone else, or some animals to get seriously hurt.

Covered wagons are made in such a way that when they are in a forward motion, the hubs that hold the wheels on are constantly being tightened. On the other hand, if you are backing up, it can be loosening the hubs.

One morning I was headed to the Hells Canyon Mule Days Parade driving Mattie and Lucie pulling my covered wagon. I had gotten the wagon out of the shed, cleaned it up and pulled it over to the corral so I could hitch the team to it.

When the team was hitched I backed them away from the corral, swung them to the side, went out through my gate and started down the county road. I went over to the corner, crossed the railroad tracks, took a sharp left, and started down Williamson Road toward town. I had gone about one hundred yards after turning the corner when all of a sudden there was a loud crash and the wagon gave a lurch as the right back corner fell to the ground. The team stopped and stood perfectly still as I got off to see what had happened. A rear wheel had come off.

I was near some neighbor's (Vernam's) driveway. They were just coming out with their team, also headed to the parade. Some of their party was in a car so they came up to see if they could help me. One of them stayed with my team as I started walking back toward home, about a half mile away, looking for the hub that held the wheel on. I found it clear back at the gate of my driveway. Mrs. Vernam had followed me in her car, so gave me a ride back to the wagon.

I always carried a wagon jack on the wagon so was able to jack up the wagon and put the wheel on again. Mrs. Vernam went on ahead to tell the parade director that I was on my way, so by the time I got there, of course everyone knew of my plight! I got to the parade staging area just as the parade was pulling out. There was no room to circle around so I just whipped in, backed up, swung my mules to the side, and was turned around. My passengers, who had been waiting patiently, loaded up and we were on our way.

I often drove the mules around the "block" for exercise. This block was a mile on each side so I drove four miles by going around it once. I lived near Hurricane Creek so there was a bridge near my house. Depending on which direction I went, I had to cross the bridge immediately, or cross it at the end of my drive.

On this particular day I decided to go in such a way that I would cross the bridge at the end of my drive. I had gone around the block having an uneventful drive, though a pretty strong wind came up while I was driving. My neighbor had hung an orange plastic tarp under the bridge to keep his cattle from walking up the creek bed under the bridge, thus getting out of his pasture. He had attached a rope to the tarp then tied the rope to the guardrail along the side of the bridge.

The wind was blowing so hard that the tarp was whipping under the bridge, causing the rope to make a popping sound as it hit against the guardrail on the side of the bridge.

As we got closer the mules became very alert. I urged them on, but the closer we got to the bridge the higher their heads became. Finally, they refused to proceed. I urged them on, talking to them soothingly. They started side stepping back and forth rather than going forward.

A strong gust of wind hit and the mules whirled to the left so sharply that they broke the tongue about two feet in front of the wagon. With the tongue broken, there was no control of the direction of the wheels. As the wheels hit things and went from side to side, this caused the broken tongue to lash from side to side. The end of the tongue was splintery and jagged, so as it whipped from side to side it hit the hind legs of the mules, cutting them severely. We ended up down in the barrow pit next to the fence.

There was blood on the road and pools of blood forming at the mules' feet. I could see the mules needed immediate attention from a vet. There was a utility pole close by so I unhitched the mules and tied them to it. I ran to my place, hooked onto the trailer, and came back for the mules.

I loaded them in the trailer and headed for the vet's. By the time I got to the vet's, which was about five miles away, the floor of the trailer was covered with blood. The vet put coagulation powder on their pasterns, wrapped their legs, and all was fine. I never again tried to drive the mules across that bridge if there was even a slight breeze!

Tom and Kelly's wedding ride

Shows convergence of Swamp and Joseph Creeks

Advertising my first book in Chief Joseph Days parade

I used the mules a few times to pack salt into some steep places for Tom Birkmaier, and pack into the Wallowa Mountains, but draft-type mules really were never meant to be pack animals. They are too big and too broad.

As time went on it seemed that I was using the mules less and less. I was no longer pulling in the Westward Ho Parade. I had quit participating in the wagon trains. I was doing very few weddings and I was doing just a couple of little parades each year. I felt the mules were being wasted. I decided to sell them while they were still young enough for someone to be interested in them.

Mattie and Lucie's new owners

After I decided to sell the mules, but before anyone had shown an interest in them, I had one more exciting adventure with them. It is a lengthy story and is told later in the chapter titled "The Call." The selling of the mules ended up being one of those "a-friend-told-a-friend-of-a-friend" deals and, a couple from south of Salt Lake City came to look at them. The man's primary concern was safety for his three small children.

Lucie and Mattie were the kind that if they knew the kids were around, the kids could go up and wrap their arms around the mule's legs and the mules wouldn't care. They were just that good! The couple bought them, took them home, then sent pictures of the kids riding them and having a good time.

Ozzie
2015-????

I started riding for Dwayne Voss on the 3V Ranch in 2013. I had ridden Chip in some steep country in the breaks of Joseph Creek so he was used to the steep country and was very surefooted.

I felt very safe when riding him in the steeper country of the lower Imnaha. As the years passed and Chip aged, it became apparent that I needed a younger horse. I knew that I needed a "canyon" horse if I were to continue to ride the steep country. I started shopping around, but could find nothing that was suitable.

'Cannon Ball' riding Ozzie

Me, riding Ozzie

In the spring of 2015 Dwayne had a couple of his horses lamed up so was short of riding horses. He brought in a little six-year-old that had been started a few years prior, but then had just been used for packing—he hadn't been ridden.

The first day I saw Ozzie (I renamed him Ozzie; while Dwayne owned him they called him Oscar.) I fell in love with him. The hired man, Will Cannon—'Cannon Ball'—rode him. Dwayne sent Cannon Ball and me up Horse Creek to ride the benches. I watched that little horse all day and by the end of the day I knew he was the horse for me! I didn't say anything to Dwayne, but in the next few weeks I watched Dwayne ride him, and then I rode him. I continued to be more and more impressed as I watched Dwayne ford the Imnaha, go through the rims, and drag calves to the fire for branding. In addition to that, while riding Ozzie, Dwayne shot his .22 Magnum with birdshot at bulls that would not come out of the brush. Dwayne also shot a .30-30 off of Ozzie! The other horses jumped sidewise when Dwayne shot the gun while riding them. Not Ozzie! It didn't bother him a bit! I rode Ozzie in some steep, nasty places and each time he impressed me!

After some time I worked up enough courage to ask Dwayne if there was any chance he would sell Ozzie to me, to which he replied, "Gosh Julie, he is my best bull-fighting horse! I can't let him go!" I said I certainly understood, but as I watched Dwayne and Cannon Ball ride him I continued to think that he should be mine. I talked to Sharon and Sherry and told them they needed to help me convince Dwayne to sell Ozzie to me. They agreed that Ozzie was just the horse for me. They told Dwayne that he and Cannon Ball were too heavy to be riding that little horse, that Ozzie was just what I needed. One morning, in the spring of 2015, as we were trailering out to start riding,

Dwayne fording Imnaha River on Ozzie

Dwayne in the rims, on Ozzie

Dwayne said, "If you really want Ozzie, I'll sell him to you!" My heart skipped a beat then when I was able to respond I said, "I don't want you to do something you will later regret. Think about it for twenty-four hours then if you still feel this way tomorrow, it's a deal!"

The next morning Dwayne said it was a deal, but he wanted to keep Ozzie through the summer and continue to ride him to be sure he was okay. I didn't really need to take possession of him until before the fall ride in October. Chip could do everything I needed of a horse until then. So that is how it happened that I became the proud owner of Ozzie!

Dwayne on Ozzie, stretching calf for branding

Dwayne on Ozzie, pulling calf to branding fire

WAGON TRAINS

I had sold the Clydesdale mares, but I still had Dick and Rocky, the Belgian geldings, and Sonny. I continued to participate in the Westward Ho Parades in conjunction with the Pendleton Round-Up, the Chief Joseph Days Parades, the Hells Canyon Mules Days activities, and many minor activities, as well as giving rides for weddings and special events.

Then in 2002 I got a call that changed my "teamster life." The Oregon Trail Interpretive Center at Baker City, Oregon was going to do a reenactment of a wagon train on part of the Oregon Trail, as a celebration of the tenth anniversary of the Center's opening.

The Center had a large old covered wagon as part of its display. They needed someone to pull it in the upcoming wagon train. An old teamster friend of mine, Gene Westberg, told them to contact me. After some consideration I decided to pull the wagon for them.

Having never participated in a wagon train before, I really did not know what to expect. When they told me that we would travel about ten miles each day, I was a little disgusted. Knowing the rate at which my team pulled my wagon on the roads around home I knew they could make ten miles in about three-and-a-half hours. I remember thinking, "My gosh, what are we going to do, drive for three or four hours then just sit around the campfire the rest of the day!"

Gene Westberg, a teamster friend of mine

Each participant was to dress in period costume. I was concerned about the hazards that wearing a long dress would impose on me as I tried to get on and off the wagon, especially if I needed to get off quickly in case of an emergency. I expressed this concern to my friend, Larry Waters. Larry and his wife, Juanita, were going to participate in the wagon train also. Larry suggested that I dress as "Calamity Jane," which I did. I was a pretty tough lookin' ol' gal in my big broad-brimmed hat, mountaineer britches and shirt, suspenders, and a six-shooter strapped to my hip!

Me, with Carolyn Witty riding "shotgun"

Carolyn Witty agreed to go and ride "shotgun" for me. Shotgun is a person who rides by the driver to give assistance as necessary. As the name implies, this person, back in pioneer times, was free to shoot while the driver drove the team. Carolyn wore cute little bonnets and long dresses each day.

I took several long dresses, thinking that I would change into them each night, to wear while sitting around the campfire, but by the time the day was

Dick and Rocky on the Oregon Trail

Wagon train on the Oregon Trail

through I was so tired I never changed into a dress except for the very last night, and then only because we got into camp early that day. I had to laugh because that last night when I was in a dress and bonnet, I was visiting with a man I had occasionally visited with throughout the week. After we had visited for about five minutes I saw "the light go on" in his eyes and he said, "Oh my gosh, that's you, isn't it Julie?"

Let me go back and tell you about that week—why it was so hard, so much work. By the end of the week I understood why the pioneers went only eight to ten miles a day! There were breakdowns and various other problems, seemingly continual. We went cross-country much of the way, on the actual Oregon Trail. Most of the way it was just a "track" out through the sagebrush.

One day we were lined out and headed down a hill. There were several teams ahead of me and I was waiting my turn. Each wagon waited until the wagon ahead of it had made it safely to the bottom, then the next wagon would start down. Often horses got tired of waiting for their turn and started messing around. This tended to end up in a wreck, or "nearly a wreck."

The team ahead of me started down the hill. As they proceeded, something broke, letting the wagon run up on the team. The team was smart—they knew to turn up hill to protect themselves. As I was waiting for the previous wagon to be repaired and gotten out of the way, my horses became impatient. Rocky was bobbing his head around, probably because of flies on his face. I was using bits that had long shanks on them.

The shank is the part of the bit that is outside the mouth and goes up along the cheek and extends down toward the chin, or below it. Somehow as Rocky was bobbing his head, he stuck one of the shanks down through the ring on the end of the neck yoke. This caused his head to be cramped in an uncomfortable position, and his mouth to be pinched by the bit.

The Bureau of Land Management had sent three of their people to act as "out riders" since we would be crossing BLM land. Some people joked that the BLM sent them along to keep us from robbing the sage hen nests and using the eggs for scrambled eggs for breakfast! Anyway, fortunately for me, two of these BLM people, Dan Thomas and Shaney Rockefeller, were close by and came to my rescue. There was so much pressure on the bit that Dan could not pull it out of the ring. After several attempts it was obvious that another plan was needed. It was decided that the pole strap had to be unsnapped to give slack to the bit so it could be pulled out of the ring.

BLM personnel

The problem was that there was so much pressure on the pole strap it could not be unsnapped. The only way to relieve some of the pressure on the pole strap was to get Rocky to tuck his head even further. Since his chin was pulled back to where it was almost against his chest it was nearly impossible to tuck it further.

I had to stay up in the wagon seat and hold the lines, so it was up to Dan and Shaney to figure it out and get it done. It was decided that Dan would reach under Rocky's belly so he could unsnap the pole strap. Shaney would stand at Rocky's head. On the count of three, Shaney would push Rocky's nose back, which would give slack to the pole strap, and Dan would quickly unsnap it. It worked as planned. Once the pole strap was unsnapped the tension was off the bit and Dan could get it out of the ring.

At times like this a well-trained, calm, sensible team is priceless. If Rocky had thrown a fit he could have caused a real wreck. He could have hurt himself, hurt some of us, and damaged the wagon and gear. Also, if Dick had not been willing to stand calmly during the whole ordeal there could have been just as big a wreck.

Finally, it was my turn to descend the hill. The wagon I was pulling was one of the heaviest, if not the heaviest of the whole lineup. The braking apparatus was not adequate. The brake stick was at the back of the wagon out of reach of the driver. There was no rope connected to the brake stick and strung to the front, where the driver could reach it, which meant I simply had no brakes. Dick and Rocky were going to have to hold it back all on their own.

Carolyn and I had become quite good friends with Dan Thomas, one of the BLM guys. Dan kept expressing his concern about my wagon having no brakes. As I prepared to start Dick and Rocky down the hill, Dan said he was going to ride right next to my wagon and operate the brake stick. He did ride by me and I could hear him say, every few seconds, "I'm right here, I'm right here Julie, I'm right here." What a relief it was to have his help! He knew just how much to apply the brakes and it worked wonderfully!

As each wagon reached the bottom of the hill the teams were allowed to rest, in preparation for the next challenge—climbing up the other side of the draw. It was quite steep and at least 150 yards long. Again we waited for our turn before starting up the hill, and again we each waited until the wagon in front of us had made it, before we proceeded. Some of the teams pulling light wagons made it to the top just fine. Others were unable to make it to the top. The team would simply stop pulling and the wagon would roll back until the driver could set the brakes. If the driver couldn't get it braked soon enough the wagon would jackknife. At that time a second team, one that had already made it to the top, would be brought down, hooked on with the original team, and the two teams would take the wagon to the top.

Other drivers didn't even try to pull the hill, but waited for a second team to come down and help them. With other teams, men riding saddle horses would use their lariat ropes to hook onto the neck yoke and help pull them to the top. Those horsemen meant well and did the best they knew how, but even at that, I saw things done that worried me and at times actually scared me!

The team just in front of me, that had a man teamster, was not able to make it on its own, but rolled backwards and jackknifed. A team came back and helped them to the top. When it was my turn, some guys came and started hooking their lariats to my neck yoke. They didn't even ask if I wanted or needed help. I figured that their thinking was, if the "man teamster" in front of me couldn't make it, there was no way a woman would make it.

Overturned wagon in gully

I told them I knew what my team could do and I thought we could make it. You could tell they were skeptical, but they backed off and let me try it. We did make it, but Dick and Rocky were really heaving by the time we got to the top. I was just glad it wasn't another hundred feet!

As we were sitting at the top letting Dick and Rocky rest I explained to Carolyn what I was seeing the horsemen do that concerned me—why I had declined their help. Just as I finished telling her this, another team and wagon made it to the top. The horsemen had again helped. They had been directly in front of the wagon, but when they got to the top, one of the riders pulled off to the side. This caused his rope to pull to the side on his saddle. The saddle was not cinched tight enough so it started to slip to the side of his horse. Thankfully the rider was quick

Cooking in Dutch ovens

thinking, so he jerked the dallies from the saddle horn just in time to keep the saddle from going under the horse's belly. As he did this he flipped the rope over his head and back onto the team. It fell down in around them and tangled around their legs. If the team had not been completely exhausted from pulling the hill it could have caused a wreck. I turned to Carolyn and said, "See what I mean?"

After pulling these steep hills, the terrain became much flatter, though it was laced with gullies. There were some people who walked the entire way. Many rode horses, and some rode in wagons. Some wanted to try driving a team, and in places it seemed safe to let them try their hand at it. Dan and Shaney both took a turn at driving Dick and Rocky. I took over the driving when we came to a dangerous place such as crossing a gully.

One man let an inexperienced woman drive his team and he didn't take the lines from her when they came to a gully. Just as a long truck has to swing wide to make it around a corner, so does a team pulling a wagon. This woman did not know this and the owner of the team apparently wasn't paying attention, so she let the team cut across the gully. The front wheel of the wagon fell into the gully and the wagon overturned, throwing out the people and contents. Fortunately, no one was seriously hurt. It did take several hours to pull the wagon up out of the gully, get it upright, gather up and reload all of its contents.

They had tried to make the whole wagon train experience as authentic as possible. All of the cooking was done over a campfire and there was no water for showers. By the end of the trip, most of us were exhausted, but I was hooked on the "wagon train experience."

Dick and Rocky pulling Gene Westberg's wagon

Several teamsters on the above-mentioned wagon train also participated in a wagon train in the Blue Mountains that was sponsored by the Pendleton Round-Up and Happy Canyon. They urged me to join that wagon train. I decided that I would join the Blue Mountain Wagon Train. At that time, I did not own a covered wagon so I borrowed one from Gene Westberg and joined the wagon train of 2003. I had such a good time that I bought my own covered wagon and continued to join the wagon train for several years. Carolyn continued to ride shotgun for me!

These wagon trains were pretty plush compared to that first wagon train. On these wagon trains in the Blue Mountains, a cook was brought in with a complete kitchen. Also an eighteen-wheeler truck with showers was provided.

These wagon trains were pretty big productions. There were between fifteen and twenty horse-drawn vehicles, the majority of which were covered wagons. There were also around one hundred horseback riders.

Carolyn holding Dick and Rocky

Circling up for the night

There were many pleasant, memory-making occurrences, which resulted in developing some lifelong friendships. Usually the worst thing to happen would be that the weather would turn bad, or something on a wagon or harness would break. Most of the teamsters brought supplies for repair of wagons or harnesses so no matter what broke, someone usually had what it took to fix it.

On rare occasions, things happened that could not be "fixed" so easily. One time we had driven/ridden all morning and had stopped for lunch. We watered our horses and let them rest for a while. Then it was time to start the afternoon drive/ride. I was sitting up in the driver's seat just waiting for the call to pull out.

Out in front of me about forty feet was a gal, Judy Salvage, who was riding a borrowed horse. She was an accomplished horsewoman who had worked on cattle ranches all her life. She was a small wiry gal who was probably in her sixties. As she started to step onto her horse, it reared and went over backwards. It was in a little depression in the ground so couldn't get its feet under it to get up. As it was thrashing around, Judy was under it the whole time. When the horse did finally get up, it stepped on her in doing so. Of course she was unconscious.

There was, in our group, a doctor and several other people with various levels of medical training. They did everything they could do for her while Vickie Leonard, who had a cell phone, rode to a ridge top to get reception and make a call for help. Vickie also had a GPS instrument so was able to not only request a helicopter, but also give a reading so they would know exactly where to come.

With a helicopter coming, they knew it was imperative that we get all of the horses and mules away from there before it arrived or we would have more accidents! Some people stayed with Judy while the rest of us headed back to camp.

They flew her to a hospital in the Tri-Cities where she remained for months! Paul Green, one of the leaders of the wagon train, said Judy never again participated in a wagon train, but she came back for a visit two years later and still was not "the same old Judy!"

On another wagon train, Brian Cook was driving right in front of me. He had a spare horse tied to the wagon and it was just following along. This horse, Tim, was a big gray Percheron that had been a stud until he was about eight years old.

After Tim was gelded, Brian started breaking him to drive, which proved to be quite a job! Tim would mule kick with both hind feet right up past the front of the wagon, almost hitting Brian in the face. By the time of the wagon train, Tim's behavior was much improved, but he still needed all the driving experience possible. Brian brought him along to trade off with one of the other horses he was driving.

Brian's wife, Carli, was riding a saddle horse off to the side of Brian's wagon. Carli was keeping her horse out away from the wagon when suddenly her horse decided it wanted to get next to the wagon. Carli tried to pull her horse away, but it simple bowed its neck and headed for the wagon. As she went past Tim, he whirled and mule kicked with both hind feet. One of his feet hit Carli on the thigh. She slid from her horse and slumped to the ground. Another gal who was riding a horse, dashed up to Carli, jumped off her horse and just dropped the reins. This horse went galloping down through all of the other riders. Randy Leonard saw all the commotion and knew something was wrong. He started back through the riders when the runaway horse ran right into him knocking him off his horse. This is an example of how a situation can escalate if everyone doesn't keep their heads and stay calm.

Carli's leg was not broken but was terribly bruised, so much so that it took months for the swelling, discoloring, and pain to go away.

Vaden with his mules   Photo by Linda Partridge

The worst wreck of all involved my friend, Vaden Floch, who was driving a nice team of mules. We were several days into the week and had been driving for several hours that morning when a team that was near the back of the line-up bolted and started to run up along the wagons ahead of it. As they ran past Vaden's team and wagon, all the noise and clattering spooked Vaden's team and they started to run too. They left the road and got out in the timber and brush where there was even rougher ground. There were rocks, gopher mounds, squirrel holes and fallen timber. A friend of Vaden's, Roger Becker, was riding shotgun for him. After a few bad jolts, Roger was thrown off in such a way that he went under the wagon and it ran over him. Vaden stayed with it for a few more bumps, but when the wagon wheels hit a small fallen tree, Vaden was thrown off too.

With no driver, the mules were free to go wherever they chose. They went through the timber and out onto a clear ridge. They were scared to death! Their blinders kept them from seeing what was behind them. All they knew was that something very noisy was right on their heels. They made a big circle and started back to where all the other teams and wagons were waiting.

Then the most unbelievable thing happened! They circled right back to where they had started and ran over Roger again. Incredibly, Roger survived! He was taken to a hospital in Walla Walla, Washington where he spent eighteen days. Everyone said he must be a tough ol' bird!

I had tied up my mules so I went to Vaden to see if he was okay. He was not seriously hurt, though he was ashen gray and so upset—worried about Roger.

Carli Cook

This whole experience completely changed my strategy of what I would do in case of a run-away. I had always been looking for ways I could maneuver through the trees, etc., to keep from hitting anything. This experience caused me to realize that the best thing to do is to run the team into something, and the quicker the better. By running them into something immediately, it gets them stopped before they get to going too fast. It probably would break the neck yoke, but that would be better than what happened to Vaden.

Regardless of how good a teamster you are, if a team decides to run, you are probably not going to be able to stop them, even if you know some old tricks like "sawing on the bit"—when you rapidly pull the lines from side to side, making the bit slide from side to side in the animal's mouth, and thus causing its head to swing from side to side.

PACK TRIPS

I have had the privilege of going on pack trips into the high Wallowas ever since I was in high school. The first trip was with our church youth group. Wayne and Meleese Cook were our chaperones, guides, packers, cooks, and whatever else was needed!

I also went on some trips with my immediate family and friends. After I was married and our kids got old enough, my husband and I, our kids—Kurt and Katrina—and another family, Doug and Kathy Marks, with their kids—Shaun and Kori—camped up the Lostine River and took day rides from camp. In the early 1980s we joined another family, the Carlsens, and went on ten-day trips for

Me, Betty Misander, Mike Stevens, *et al*

Kori Marks, Katrina and Kurt

Katrina and Kurt

Swamp Lake

several years. On those ten-day trips, we would not move camp more than twice. We didn't want to spend all of our time packing and moving. Instead, we set up a base camp and took day rides to nearby lakes and places of interest.

Probably the two most eventful mountain trips I ever took were a trip in 1989 with the Carlsens, and in 1992 when Dave and Janine Caudle, with three of their friends from Canada, came down and went to the mountains with Lee and me. The stories of these two trips can be found in *My Life on Joseph Creek*.

Camp in the lake basin—Matterhorn in the background

Drainage of Glacier Lake

Glacier Lake

Roger, Kurt, Katrina and me at Six-Mile

Dropping into N. Fork of Imnaha

Tenderfoot Basin

Kids swimming in south fork of the Imnaha River

Moving camp

Carolyn Witty and Tammy Crawford were a couple of gals who taught at the Enterprise School at the same time I was teaching there. We decided that we wanted to pack into the Snake River. Memorial Day weekend of 1989 was the chosen date because it was a four-day weekend. We each had our own horse/mule to ride and Carolyn had a horse we could pack.

We trailered to the Freeze-Out Trail Head and packed in from there. Carolyn was the only one of us who had been there before so she led the way. The trail went up over the Freeze-Out Saddle and down the other side to the benches. As we started north along the benches Carolyn said that it didn't seem right. She remembered going down a canyon.

We turned around and started back. We hadn't gone far when we discovered our mistake. The trail that went down the canyon came onto the "bench trail" at such an angle that we couldn't see it through the brush as we passed it the first time. It was easy to spot as we rode back, so down Saddle Creek we went—and all was well.

At the mouth of Saddle Creek was a large alluvial plain, so it was an excellent place to camp—a flat place for the tent and an abundance of horse feed. We were above the Snake River by quite a bit so had a real vantage point to watch jet boats and rafts go by. As the people went by, generally they would wave and shout greetings; we returned their greetings.

The week before we packed in, the senior class from Enterprise went on their annual float trip on the Snake River. They put in upriver at the Hells Canyon Dam. When they had gotten to the sandy bar at Saddle Creek they came ashore.

Many places where there were sandy beaches, the sand went out into the river a ways then dropped straight off. One of the boys who didn't know how to swim had taken his life jacket off. He was being cautious and planned to just wade out to about knee-deep water. He took a few steps then stepped over the edge and was gone in a split second.

When we were there, his body had not yet been found. Being a small town and small school, we all had taught and/or knew him. This "clouded" our trip. His body was found some time later downriver quite a ways.

Tammy Crawford ad Carolyn Witty at Freeze-out Saddle

Tammy and Carolyn headed for the Snake River

Looking up Snake River and our camp

Natural salt lick along trail

For years Carolyn and I went on four-day pack trips into the mountains. One time we packed into Francis Lake. I had heard that the fishing was wonderful so I took an extra pack animal just to pack in an inflatable raft.

One day I gathered up all of the necessary fishing gear, pumped up the raft, gave my camera to Carolyn so she could take pictures of me out there on the lake hauling in all of those fish. Right!

I paddled like mad and got out in the middle of the lake just as a stiff breeze came up and pushed me to the north end of the lake. I wasn't to be defeated easily, so I paddled toward the south end of the lake. I figured the breeze would then push me toward the north end again—it would be like trolling, without the noise of a motor. Perfect!

Francis Lake

Sometimes it seems nature gets its kicks out of playing tricks on us—it sure seemed that was the case that day! Just as I almost reached the south end of the lake, the direction of the breeze changed and washed me up on the south shore. Again I was determined to make this work. After all, I had brought an extra mule just to pack this raft—I was going to use it! I waited a little while to see if the wind was going to change directions again. After waiting for some time I decided

Me, with raft on Francis Lake

that the wind must have made up its mind to blow from the north. I paddled toward the north end of the lake, again figuring if I could make it to the north end I would "troll" back to the south. I was tiring from all of the rowing, but I was persistent! Well, about the time I got to the north end, the wind changed again. I was whipped! I was ready to give up! The north end did not have a good place to go to shore so I paddled back toward the south end where I could get out. I was so exhausted I could hardly make it to shore. I packed that raft out of the mountains simply because I didn't want to "litter" by leaving it there on the lakeshore. I have never even considered using the thing again!

My cousin Lyle had for years wanted to retrace the route his mother had taken as a little girl when her dad had packed them from Cow Creek to Buckhorn each spring, then from Buckhorn back to Cow Creek each fall.

Lyle by original Clemons cabin remains. Second cabin in back

Lyle in front of Clemons cabin

Joe Clemons, Lyle's grandfather, had homesteaded at Buckhorn. He ran a few cows and summered them up around Buckhorn, then took them into the canyon for the winter. He had a little cabin at the mouth of Cow Creek and one at Buckhorn. Mr. Clemons would even take the sewing machine apart so it could be carried on a pack animal, thus Mrs. Clemons could sew all year long! Joe and his wife, Edith, had three girls: Josephine, Mary and Ruth. The girls went to school at Rim Rock, which was up the Imnaha River just past the mouth of Fence Creek. Josephine and Ruth each married Simmons boys who became sheep and cattle ranchers on the Imnaha.

Mary married my dad's brother, Don, and they lived on down Joseph Creek three miles from where I was raised. Mrs. Clemons was a quarter Indian and knew a lot of Indian history, which she passed on to her girls and their families. She told the story of how Cemetery Ridge got its name. Cemetery Ridge was just north of the Clemons's cabin at Buckhorn. There was a draw on the west side of Cemetery Ridge, which drained into Cherry Creek. At the head of the draw was a good spring, so the "Wallowa Indians" of the Nez Perce tribe often camped there.

Indian grave on Cemetery Ridge

The "Snake Indians," from over on the Snake River, would often ambush the Wallowa Indians. One time the Snake Indians climbed up out of the Imnaha Canyon in the dark of night and hid under the rims at the top of Cemetery Ridge. At daybreak they attacked the Wallowa Indians—there was a death loss on both sides. When the battle was over, the Wallowa Indians buried their dead at the head of the little draw. They dug as deep as they could with their crude digging tools, put the bodies in and covered them with dirt.

Me on Chip, overlooking Snake River

They then packed rocks from the nearby hillside and covered the graves with mounds of rocks. Over one hundred years later, rectangular mounds of rocks could be seen where these burials took place. The Snake Indians also buried their dead under the cliffs by piling huge mounds of rocks on the bodies. I am sure the Indians would have named the place 'Something' Burial Ground but the white man named it Cemetery Ridge.

In 2008 I told Lyle I would pack him in to this country. I had Mattie and Lucie to use as pack animals and I could ride Chip. I asked Carolyn Witty if I could borrow her horse, Cricket, for Lyle to ride.

We trailered to the trailhead on Cemetery Ridge, packed up and headed down the old Eureka Road. This road had been built in the early 1900s so supplies could be taken into the mining community of Eureka. A complete account of this can be found in *Snake River in Hells Canyon*, by Johnny Carry, Cort Conley, and Ace Barton.

Lyle riding up the Imnaha Trail

It was easy going until we dropped into the bottom of Eureka Creek—also called Deer Creek— where it became very brushy in places. It was hard to find the trail through the brush.

We set up camp on a little bench above the Snake River, near the remains of the Eureka mining facility. It had been a long day so we pitched our tents, ate a light supper and went to bed.

The next morning, we saddled the horses, tied the mules to a hackberry bush then rode down to Eureka Bar and the Imnaha Rapids. There was still a pile of ore that was supposed to be shipped out, but with the sinking of the *Imnaha* the whole mining venture collapsed so rapidly that the ore was left behind. A complete story of Eureka can be found in *Snake River in Hells Canyon*, by Carrey, Conley and Barton.

Remains of Eureka mining operation

When the *Imnaha* sank, it turned sidewise in the river. It hung up on the cliff on one side of the river and on huge rocks on the other. Lyle's granddad, Joe Clemons, was on the boat. He and the rest of the men were able to jump onto the huge rocks and save themselves.

We poked around the area for a couple of days and Lyle fished, then we broke camp and headed up the Imnaha Trail. At places, the poison ivy was higher than our heads when we were on our horses! The blackberry vines had encroached onto the trail so badly that in places the horses resisted going through them. They wanted to step around them and there was no trail to step around on! At the mouth of Cow Creek, we could look across the river and see the tailings of Joe Clemons's mines. He had three mines. The names of two of them were Morning Star and Evening Star. Lyle couldn't remember the name of the third one.

Lyle examining ore

Once we reached Cow Creek we were on the trail that Lyle's mom had ridden as a child. We went up a draw to the Tully Creek benches then took the north fork of Tully Creek. This trail went around under Spain Saddle and topped out on the Eureka Road. We had made a circle, and never saw a snake!

Me, looking down Snake River

Snake Canyon to left, Imnaha to right

The Tully Place

Lyle, across the river from Joe Clemons mine tailings

Cabin on Eureka Creek

Tully Creek Trailhead. Lightning Creek to left, Horse Creek to the right. Seven Devils in far distance

Topping out of Tully Creek. Spain saddle in background

Jim Larsen, headed for Burger Pass

Headed down into Elk Creek

Brian Cook

Vicki Leonard

When I participated in the wagon trains I made a lot of friends. A couple of them liked packing into the mountains as much as I did. They were Brian Cook from Irrigon and Vickie Leonard from Pendleton. We talked about going into the mountains for several years before it finally happened.

In August of 2011 we met near La Grande, then went up Katherine Creek, out of Union, to the Buck Creek trail head. We packed up and headed up the trail. Brian had brought a friend, Jim Larsen, with him.

We had gone a mile or so when we had to cross a little creek. The animals were thirsty after being hauled for several hours and climbing up the mountain. As each of us crossed the creek we let our saddle horses and pack animals drink, then we would pull ahead so the next person could water his animals.

Brian watered his animals and pulled up then Jim watered his animals and pulled up. On the far side of the creek was a small, relatively steep bank. Jim couldn't see the pack animal that was last in the string, so he didn't realize that he had not gone far enough to get this animal past the bank. As he was waiting for Vickie to get her animals watered, his pack animals were stepping around. The back one stepped back and put his foot over the edge of the bank. He jerked back, yanking on the pack animal he was tied to. They all started jumping around, causing one of the packs to slip. The pack had to be reset before we went on. We were fortunate that no mules rolled!

We crossed over Burger Pass and headed down into the drainage of Elk Creek. Brian had hunted in this area so knew of a good place to camp down in Elk Creek.

Things were going smoothly when all of a sudden one of Brian's pack mules started bucking. He broke loose from the string and came bucking back around the mountainside toward Vickie and me and our animals.

This mule was carrying "the kitchen" so all of the cooking utensils, pots and pans, tableware, etc., were scattered all over the mountainside. The "good thing" was the fact that this happened at the only place along the trail where the mule could throw a fit and not go into a roll. Anywhere else the mule would have rolled to his death!

Camp in Elk Creek

Camp in Elk Creek

We gathered up all of the supplies the best we could, tied the mule in the string then headed on to the campsite. We set up a comfortable camp, had supper, and went to bed. We rose the next morning after a good night's sleep. We saddled our horses, and a couple of pack animals to pack the fishing gear, then headed up to Tombstone Lake and some much-awaited fishing. Brian and Vickie had brought fishing tubes, so were able to get out on the lake and do some good fishing. Jim caught a few from the shoreline and I caught just one.

On the way up to the lake, Brian explained that it was customary for the person who caught the fewest fish to buy ice cream for everyone when we got back to town. That's what they do on all of his fishing trips!

I tried to talk my way out of it by pleading that it was like hitting a guy when he's down! I already felt so bad about not catching fish and now they were going to make me *buy them ice cream!* What kind of a deal was this!? Ha!

Brian fishing in Tombstone Lake

When we were ready to leave the mountains and head home, we discovered that Vickie's pack mule was lame. We were able to split up his load and put it on the other pack animals. He didn't want to travel so was going really slow. Vickie and I talked the guys into going on and we would come at a slower pace. The mule would go if I stayed right on his tail. I don't know if he was afraid of Chip or thought I was going to pop him with the end of a rope. It was totally against the way Brian thinks and does things, to go off and leave "the girls," but we finally persuaded him. He knew we were capable.

Vickie and me at Burger pass

We all decided that we had had such a great time that we were going to do it every year that we possibly could. Of course, they REALLY enjoyed the ice cream!

For our mountain trip in 2014 we decided to go up the Lostine River and take the Bowman trail in to the North Minam Meadows. We were to meet at the trailhead. Brian came from Irrigon and brought a friend, Dave Hendricks, with him. Vickie came from Pendleton. As all of them came through Wallowa they noticed that Bear Creek was a muddy torrent, and extremely high for that time of year.

We met as planned, packed up, and started up the trail. We were pleased to find that a place on the trail that had been so bad it could have been classified as "treacherous" the last time I was over it, had been repaired. It was fixed so well we couldn't even tell the exact spot where it had been.

When we got to the back end of Brownie Basin, we started coming across places in the trail where sand and small gravel had washed down from the mountainside above. The farther we went the worse it got. We zigzagged up the switchbacks, coming to places where there was more and more sand in the trail, and places where the trail was completely washed away. Just under the top, along the last switchback, the trail was across an area that was just sand—there were no rocks to hold the sand in place. Some places we could see traces of the trail; at other places the trail was completely gone.

Trail washed out near Wilson Pass

We were relieved to make it to the top, Wilson Pass. We rested the animals as we enjoyed the beauty all around us. We checked cinches then started down the other side, dropping into Wilson Basin. Almost immediately the trail became substantially worse. We could tell that a real "gully washer" had "dumped" here. In places there were gullies, washed down to bare rock; in other places the gullies were full of large boulders and debris that had washed down from above.

There were places where hikers could not walk, but instead had to take their packs off, throw them ahead, then scoot and crawl through the rocks, until they reached their packs. They would then have to throw the packs again, and again crawl to them. They had to keep repeating this until they got to the other side of the wash. We understood why Bear Creek was running such a torrent! It was a miracle that we did not break an animal's leg going through that! We finally reached the bottom—North Minam Meadows.

The meadow was full of grass up to the horses' knees. There was evidence of just one camp prior to us. We had the meadow all to ourselves! This was unusual. We had a great campsite and the horse feed was abundant. We settled in for a few days of relaxation and fun.

Camp in North Minam Meadows

Years before, when we went to the mountains, we avoided North Minam Meadows because that was where everyone went. By mid-August all of the horse feed would be gone and the campsites were trampled into a bed of dust.

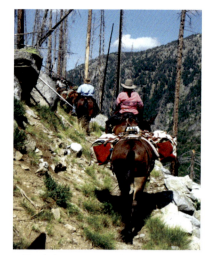
Headed into Green Lake

Me, Brian, and Dave

Fishing on Green Lake

Vickie on Bowman Trail

I think the lack of use of the mountains can be attributed primarily to two things. First, it seems there are fewer and fewer people who know how to pack animals and "horse camp." Secondly, the lack of maintenance of the trails discourages people. Riders don't want to break the leg of a horse or mule, but it is not just the "horse people" who are discouraged; backpackers carrying their heavy packs get tired of having to crawl over rocks and debris.

The day after arriving in the meadows, we rode up to Green Lake for some fishing. It required a substantial amount of trail work. The trail had not been cleared for years so there were a lot of trees across it. We were fortunate that the trail itself was in pretty good shape.

As was customary, Brian, Vickie, and Dave brought fishing tubes, so after gearing up they headed for the middle of the lake. All three of them had some great fishing. Again I didn't catch many from the shore, but hiked all the way around the lake and had a very enjoyable day.

The fishing had been so good that the guys decided that they wanted to go back to Green Lake the next day. Before they started fishing that day, we took a count of how many fish each of us would eat for the next supper and breakfast. They agreed to keep just that number of fish. We didn't want to pack any out, and we didn't want to waste any. They didn't fish long until they had the agreed-upon number of fish, so the rest of the day was spent in "catch and release."

As I had hiked around the lake the day before, I had seen a lot of huckleberries, so this second day I brought a Ziploc bag for berries. I picked enough berries to make syrup for breakfast the next morning. I had taken some sugar to sweeten my tea so I used it to make the syrup. Brian said it was the best huckleberry syrup he had ever eaten—things always taste better in the mountains!

As the day approached when we had to leave, we were dreading it for two reasons. First we didn't want to leave the mountains, and secondly, we were dreading going through those bad places on the trail.

Since the worst places were just up the trail from North Minam Meadows, we would get the worst behind us at the beginning of the trip out. We were glad for that. Also, we knew that it was easier going up through bad spots than it was to go down. We made it out without incident, loaded up, and started for home. The rest of them would have to go through Wallowa so they decided to stop at The Little Bear for a burger. I followed them down so we could have one last visit and say our goodbyes. They wouldn't let me pay for their burgers, though I was again the loser in the fishing contest. I guess I redeemed myself with the huckleberry syrup!

TRAIL RIDES

Asotin to Joseph

The Asotin to Joseph Trail Ride was advertised as "A Hundred Mile Ride for A Hundred Riders." It started at the Asotin Fair Grounds in Asotin, Washington and ended at Joseph, Oregon at the time of the Chief Joseph Rodeo and celebration, the last full weekend of July.

The first ride was in July of 1990, to celebrate the Asotin County Fair's 50th anniversary. The ride was held, not all, but most of the following years with the ride the summer of 2006 being its eleventh and final ride. I was fortunate enough to participate in the last two rides, 2005 and 2006.

We met at the Fair Grounds where a dinner was provided for us. Those who had come some distance camped at the fairgrounds. Others, who lived close by, went home after the dinner and returned early the next morning. There were many people who had participated in previous Asotin to Joseph rides so knew the agenda and timeline. We first-timers were waiting with anticipation.

Vaden Floch was the trail master for the first segment of the trip; Wayne Tippett was the trail master for the second segment. I had become friends with Vaden and Heather through my participation in the Wagon Trains in the Blue Mountains. It was through this acquaintance and friendship that I heard about the trail ride.

Looking down on Asotin, Washington Clarkston in the distance

Vaden and Heather kept commenting that if people could make the first hill, they probably could make the trip. When I saw the "first hill" I couldn't understand their concern. It was an open hillside, which wasn't very steep, and there were no rims or cliffs to be concerned about.

Along the breaks of the Snake River

When Vaden gave the call to "move out" that first morning, we rode out of the fairgrounds, crossed the highway, and started up the hill southeast of Asotin. We had not gone a quarter of a mile when a man had to reset his saddle; another guy let his horse go up the wrong side of a little draw so the horse became nervous as the other horses got farther and farther away from him. The man got off and walked, leading the horse.

We climbed higher until we were above the water tower for the town of Asotin. We had gone approximately half a mile and had stopped for photos of the beautiful landscape below. I looked down, and sure enough, several people had turned back.

We made our way along the breaks of the Snake River. It was breath taking to see the river far below. That night we camped at Vaden and Heather's ranch, which was partially on the breaks, but mostly out on top. Because of my friendship with Vaden and Heather, and because I was so interested in the history of the country we would be riding through, I rode at the front with them so I could ask Vaden questions.

By the time we got to the Floch ranch, one lady and her daughter were exhausted. It was much harder than they had anticipated so they decided to drop out. It probably is a good thing because the next day's ride was much more challenging.

It was July, so at times it was quite warm, but nothing unbearable. Each night a camp was set up on a road where it was possible to bring in an eighteen-wheeler truck with showers. The meals were all catered, so a cook and his crew brought in all the necessary vehicles and supplies to provide wonderful meals.

Vaden Floch, Grand Ronde below

Most of the participants of the ride had support staff who shuttled their rigs to each campsite. A lot of the people slept in their horse trailers, but some had campers or motor homes. Those of us without a support crew threw our belongings into a truck, which brought them to each campsite. We put up tents, if we had not been invited to sleep in someone's horse trailer.

The horse feed was provided. Riders tied their horses to their horse trailers and/or put up an electric fence to make a small lot for their horses so they could move around during the night, rather than having to stand in one place.

Me overlooking juncture of Snake and Grand Ronde Rivers

On the second day of the ride we left the Floch Ranch and continued along the breaks of the Snake River. As we went along, Vaden told one story after another of the adventures and experiences of many of his ancestors and immediate family who had homesteaded and ranched in that area. Some of the old homestead buildings were still standing, but barely.

Most days, our lunch was brought to us by someone in a pickup. If we were somewhere that was inaccessible by vehicle, we would carry our lunches with us on our horses. The second day, right after lunch, we were going to head down the "mail trail."

Mountain sheep on point below us!

This trail had been used for years to deliver mail to the people down on the Grande Ronde River and the Snake River before roads were built along the rivers. The trail had also been traveled extensively by people going to social events. The people on the rivers would ride up to Anatone for a dance or some other event then ride back into the canyon in the dark of night, unless they danced 'til dawn!

Horseshoe Bend of Grand Ronde River

We camped on the Grande Ronde the second night. It was quite warm, so a few people took their horses swimming. Chip had never been in deep water so I just took him "wading." I got him into water up to his knees and he just stood there, so I started splashing water on myself and on him. He stood there for a little longer then suddenly he started striking the water. He would strike with one front foot until that leg tired then he would strike with the other. Each time his hoof hit the water it would make a "pop" almost as loud as a small gun. He splashed water on himself, and me, until he was exhausted. As he was playing in the water, I kept leading him into deeper and deeper water until he could no longer strike. The water was up to his belly. He seemed to really enjoy it!

Fording Grand Ronde River

The next day we had to ford the Grande Ronde. The place we chose was quite wide, so not very deep. I was second in line to enter the river. The lead horse decided he did not want to go in. After several attempts, the rider said, "Julie, see if your horse will go in." Chip stepped right in and we headed across. I know Chip would not have been so willing if he had not "played" in the water the night before.

Wayne Tippett

After we crossed the river we were headed for "my country"—the Joseph Creek country! Wayne Tippett became the trail boss at this point. Wayne's family had ranched in the lower Joseph Creek area for several generations. They also had ranches in other canyons, and in the hill lands of Wallowa County.

Again I stuck close to the Trail Boss, Wayne, so I could get many of my questions answered as we proceeded up the Grande Ronde, Joseph Creek, Cottonwood, and Horse Creek. This is a different Horse Creek than the one on Imnaha at Dwayne's place. We left Horse Creek and

Looking north across the Grand Ronde Canyon from Wallowa County

started up Trail Creek, which took us to the top, and The Frog Ponds. There was an old logging road up this canyon.

At lunchtime everyone tied their horse to a tree or bush along the side of the road. After lunch we mounted and were ready to head on up the canyon. Vaden was riding a great little mare that had a lot of training. Vaden could make her side step as she was walking up the road simply by using leg pressure, so when he had mounted and nudged her to start walking and she didn't respond, he was quite surprised. He tried a couple more times, to no avail then he looked down and saw that he had not untied her lead rope from the bush.

He quickly dismounted and looked around to see if anyone had noticed. Of course I had and I was grinning from ear to ear! Vaden was flustered, so he quickly untied the mare and remounted. He nudged the mare, but again she would not move. Vaden knew I was watching the whole thing and that I would "get a lot of miles out of this one."

At this point Vaden was embarrassed! He looked at the lead rope again and saw that it was still wrapped around a branch of the bush he had tied to. So he got off again, unwrapped the rope, remounted, and away we went! I was chuckling all the time!

A couple of nights later, around the campfire at Thomason Meadows, I did a pantomime of the whole episode!

I also wrote the following poem and read it another night. I introduced it as something Vaden had written and I just happened to come across it!

For the Shape I'm In

There's really nothing the matter with me,
I'm about as healthy as a man can be.

My Doc says my liver is plumb out of whack,
I suffer tremendously from this pain in my back.

My teeth are failing me, that's why I don't grin,
But I'm in FAIR shape for the shape I'm in.

I walk so slow my dog nips at my heels,
But when I try to speed up, this ol' body rocks and reels.

I have severe arthritis in most every joint,
So me attempting to run, well, there's really no point.

My eyes are full of matter, they stick shut every night,
The first thing in the morning, I look quite a fright!

I don't spend much on shampoo, my hair is so thin,
But I'm in FAIRLY GOOD shape, for the shape I'm in!

My back has a hump and my legs are all bowed,
As I walk down the street, I look like a toad.

My toes are all gnarled, sticking out in 10 different ways,
It's an understatement to say they've seen better days.

The chest I used to stick out with pride,
Has become a big paunch, which I now try to hide.

My eyes aren't what they used to be, my sight is quite dim,
But I'm in GOOD shape, for the shape I'm in!

My hearing's so poor I have to say, "Repeat that please,"
And when I talk, I speak with a wheeze.

My nose constantly runs and my feet smell like rot,
My armpits are so hairy, they're tied in a knot.

My pulse is very weak, my blood extremely thin,
But I'm in DARNED GOOD shape, for the shape I'm in!

My snoring's so bad it keeps my wife awake all through the night,
With my mouth drooped open, drooling, I'm really quite a sight.

My faithful ol' horse, she takes pity on me,
She can tell I sure ain't the cowboy I used to be!

My memory has left me, my head's in a spin,
But you know what? I'm in EXCELLENT shape, for the shape I'm in!

Our next camp was at Biden and Casey Tippett's out in the Zumwalt area, near "The Buttes." An auction was held that night, with proceeds going to the Asotin County Fair Boosters. Businesses and individuals donated items. Some of the most popular were miniature barns, corrals, etc. made by Casey.

The ride continued toward the Wallowa Valley—the goal being to make it to Joseph by Friday night, then ride in the Chief Joseph Days Parade on Saturday morning. We made it to the parade and made a quite impressive entry with all of our riders—one hundred riders and horses! We had ridden one hundred miles to get there!

I have to tell you about Vaden. He was one of those guys who never had an enemy—everyone who knew him liked him! I never, ever, heard anyone say even one bad thing about him. And, oh how he loved to tease! I like to tease too, so Vaden and I were always trying to get one up on each other. I tell you, you would have to "get up early" to get ahead of Vaden! I never did.

He also was the catalyst for many fun times with his family and friends. He was the one always saying, "Hey, let's go..." He was all heart, but he had a bad heart—we lost him on January 21, 2012. He will be sorely missed!

Day Rides

Not all trail rides were as elaborate as the Asotin to Joseph ride. One-day rides took a lot less preparation and scheduling. I've always loved "playing" guide and taking people into some of my favorite places.

In the spring before the snow had receded enough to go into the mountains, I liked to ride in the hill country. One of my favorite places was the old Swamp Creek Cow Camp. I went into it on the Chico Trail.

The Chico Trail was an excellent trail to ride colts on because there were no rims of cliffs to worry about. A horse could get on and off the trail any place without the worry of getting into trouble. It was an easy trail, so was good for those first rides in the spring when a person was wanting to "leg a horse up," which means getting your horse in condition.

A lot of the lakes and mountain country required more than a day's ride to get to them. To see those required a pack trip, but there were quite a few lakes in the mountains that were close enough to ride into, have lunch, and come back out the same day.

Ival & Wayne Clark on face of Mt. Joseph

Me, at Maxwell Lake

Wayne, Ival & Katrina out of Swamp Creek Cow Camp

Me on Jake, Jessica on Doc in McCully Basin

Echo Lake

Blanche Maxwell on Doc, Copper Creek Trail above Swamp Lake

Copper Creek Trail blocked with snow above Swamp Lake

On Copper Creek Trail

Blanche at Maxwell Lake

Katrina and Lee in Tenderfoot Basin

Thorpe Basin

Jody Coggins, Debbie Weebe, Katrina

Me, with Chip at Chimney Lake

Chimney Lake from trail to Hobo Lake

Jessica at Falls Creek

Jessica on Duke, Sacajawea Peak behind

Me, on the edge of Hobo Lake

Vaden and Heather Floch, Carolyn and Ken Witty at Chimney Lake

Carolyn and Ken Witty, Vaden and Heather Floch at Laverty Lakes

Marr Flat Cattle Company

As I talked with Todd Nash of my grandparents having homesteaded on Marr Flat, he detected my keen interest in that part of the country. I asked him if I could help him move cattle sometime—he said I could. He also invited me to help with a branding.

It was the spring of 2005 when he called and said he was going to be branding some calves in the Kiser corrals at the head of Rail Canyon. It is in the general vicinity of the Three Buck area, on the way to The Cat's Back and The Divide. He wondered if I would like to help. Of course I would! From the time I was a little girl, there was always something special about branding day! We went out early to gather the cattle, and had them to the corral before the rest of the branding crew arrived.

At Kiser Corrals

Me, giving shots

Later that same spring, Todd called again and said he was going to be moving some cattle from The Divide down into Big Sheep and wondered if I would like to help.

Chip, my main horse, was laid up with an injury, so I had to ride another horse I had recently purchased. The horse turned out to be a dud so I sold him shortly thereafter. Because of the lack of "horse power" I was not as much help as I would have liked to have been. Scott Shears, from the Triple Creek Ranch, also helped that day. We gathered the cattle off The Divide, put them through a gate, and started around the hill to the ridge we would push the cattle down. There had been a fence along that hillside in the past, but at this time all that was left was the wire. It was strung all over the hillside, going across the trail in some places. This made it difficult to keep the horses from getting tangled in it, and cut by the wire. I didn't have dogs at that time so was limited in my effectiveness.

The cattle had to go just beyond the ridge and down through a trough between two rims and grade back out onto the point of the ridge. Then they graded down to the bottom of the Big Sheep Canyon. We let them mother-up for a while then headed for the top. My horse proved to be less than satisfactory when driving the cattle down into the canyon, and I was unhappy with him. I actually had to lead him some of the way! I decided that rascal was going to at least pack me out of there, and he did.

I expressed my dissatisfaction with the horse's performance to Todd and Scott. Scott was kind in saying, "Well, he just isn't snappy." He could have said, "I think he's a dud!"

Anyway, it was a fun day and I got to see some new country—the Dixie Jet—and ride where I hadn't ridden before. The guys were patient, and it was a great day!

Heading for Big Sheep Creek

It was the spring of 2007, and time for Todd to trail cattle from the valley to Big Sheep Creek. It would be a three-day drive. The first day, we drove the cattle across the valley and put them in a pasture at the forks of the Zumwalt and Crow Creek Roads.

Dropping into Big Sheep

The second day would be a long one, with the destination being a holding lot down in the Little Sheep Creek canyon, along the Imnaha Highway. Knowing it would be a long day, Todd had us in the saddle before 6:00 a.m. We trailed the cattle to the top of OK Gulch then took a lane east that took us into Dwayne Voss's pastures.

Todd Nash and Scott Shear

We crossed Dwayne's land then dropped into the South Fork of Lightning Creek. There were lots of riders, so the cattle were pretty much kept in the bottom of the draw. We trailed through the extensive feed lot of the Lightning Creek Ranch, past the enormous hay shed—the length of two football fields—then down the Lightning Creek Road to the Imnaha Highway. By the time we pushed the last of the cattle off the highway and into the holding lot, it was getting dusk and we were concerned that a vehicle might come along and not be able to see the cattle. We all breathed a sigh of relief when the last cow was off the highway

Going across Three Lakes country

Heading down main Lightning Creek

South fork of Lightning Creek

Lightning Creek Ranch feed bunks

Lightning Creek Ranch hay shed

PART TWO
RIDING FOR THE BIRKMAIER RANCH

Getting Started

It was 2003—and now that I owned my own saddle horse—Chip—I felt qualified to "hang out my shingle" for day riding. My first thought was, that since I knew the Monument Ranch range so well, I could do a good job of riding that country. I approached the guy who was then running cattle there, but he quickly dismissed me.

Next, I approached Tom Birkmaier of the Birkmaier Ranch on Crow Creek and Joseph Creek. Tom was the age of my kids—they actually played together when they were little. Sometimes when I was riding on my husband's and my ranch on Joseph Creek I would drop my kids off and they would spend the day playing with Tom. Tom's older sister, Lorri, would "babysit" them.

Tom had grown up, married, and had two little girls. He now lived in the ranch house there on Crow Creek, as his parents, Mack and Marion, had moved to the valley and lived at their place on Walker Lane, near Joseph.

I had never ridden Tom's pastures, and it had been a long time since I rode the Cougar Creek and Swamp Creek ranges. I had a lot of new pastures to learn. You don't really know a pasture until you have ridden it, learned all of its water holes, salt licks, trails, and the location of gates.

We all carried radios so we could talk back and forth. When learning a new pasture, it was a great help to be able to get ahold of Tom and get instructions on which way to go, etc. Tom knew all of that country as well as he knew the back of his hand. I could call him and describe my surroundings. Tom would think for a moment then come on the radio and tell me what to do and where to go. Tom was patient with me as I was learning the country. He knew I was doing my best, and that's all he asked. After riding for Tom for a couple of years and having an opportunity to learn the lay of the land, he came to realize I really could be of some help and was not just a woman who needed to be "babysat." He found he could send me off by myself to move or gather cattle. This freed him to do other things he needed to do.

At about that time, Tom and his wife split up and she moved out of the county. Tom had his girls a lot and he took them with him wherever he went. He had a couple of good old horses that the girls rode. When we were gathering cattle, the girls would go with us all day. They were tough little shavers; they amazed me!

Aspen, Chloe, Bud Birkmaier, Cory Miller, Tom

If we got into a situation that required some fast, difficult riding, one of us would stay with the girls and the other would go after the cattle. As the girls got older, it got easier and easier.

One day we were riding on the Cougar Creek range. There was a fence running along the breaks of Sumac. When we came to the gate, there was a calf elk tangled in the wire of the gate. The wire was wrapped around its front leg and had cut the skin. Tom loosed the calf, but it just lay there.

I almost always carried a camera with me and that day was no exception so I took pictures of Aspen and Chloe kneeling behind the calf elk.

The cattle were scattering so I hurried off to gather them while Tom and the girls started off in another direction. As they were leaving, a coyote started howling close by, so Tom went back to the calf, walking all around it, leaving as much human scent as possible, hoping it would ward off the coyote. It was then that they heard a cow elk calling from a nearby draw. Tom was confident the calf would be okay!

Tom, Aspen and Chloe

Bud, Chloe and Aspen

One of Tom's dogs, that none of us will probably ever forget, was old Brownie. He had a lot of grit. When he got after a cow, she moved! The only trouble with Brownie was that he was a fighter. He was always trying to lord over the other dogs and pick a fight.

Mack said he was the only dog they ever bought. He got him from the Snyders, who lived out in the

Aspen and Chloe with calf elk

Flora area, and paid $25 for him. Mack took him home to his place on Walker Lane, near Joseph, but Brownie wouldn't stay home. He would go to a neighbor's, Joe Zinni's place, because Joe kept food out for his dogs all the time. Mack would go over to bring Brownie home, but Brownie would crawl under a shed and stay just far enough from the hole that Mack couldn't get a hold of him. Mack lost patience with the whole situation and sent Brownie to the ranch and told Tom to keep him!

When at the ranch on Crow Creek, Brownie continued his old habit of not staying home. Often he would go several miles down Joseph Creek to Bob Lathrop's. Bob had been having trouble with a cougar prowling around his calving lot. One night he was on his ATV checking cattle in the middle of the night. He didn't know Brownie was anywhere around. Brownie liked riding with Tom on the ATV so when he heard Bob's ATV he ran toward it. As Bob saw eyes coming at him in the dark, he thought it was the cougar. It all happened so fast that Bob didn't realize it was Brownie until Brownie was in his lap. Bob said it was the most scared he had ever been in his entire life!

Brownie started wandering even farther. He would leave the ranch on Crow Creek and go to the valley, over thirty miles away. One time he wandered into a place on Green Valley Road, near where the old livestock auction barn had been. The people who lived there had killed an elk, and hung it in a shed. It was common practice to let meat hang for a week or more, if the weather was cool, before cutting and wrapping the meat. Because of this, the people had no reason to check on the meat.

Apparently Brownie had been helping himself to the meat for several days before the people discovered him. He had eaten both hindquarters and most of the loins. Tom said that when he went to get Brownie, he was so full of meat he looked like he was about to pop!

As Brownie got older and it got harder for him to get around and jump up on the back of the pickup, I started asking Tom to leave him home. Tom would say, "Oh let him go, he wants to go."

Brownie is with me on the breaks of Swamp Creek.

I especially remember one time, toward the end, when Brownie went along with us to move cattle. For some reason he ended up going along with me. That day we were gathering Sumac. The first pasture we rode consisted of canyons and draws that headed up on Red Hill and emptied into Sumac.

As I zigzagged up a south hillside to get to the top of a ridge, old Brownie cut across so he could keep up with me. He never trotted along, but methodically put one foot in front of the other. I took my time so the old fellow could keep up. When I got to the top of the ridge, and along the breaks of the next "north"—the side of the canyon that faces north and is usually covered with brush and timber—I looked across to the next south hillside. There were cattle on it, pretty close to the top.

On the ridge I was on, there was a lone bull. He knew the cows were just across the canyon so he baled off into the canyon, crashing his way down through the timber and brush. He could go much faster than me so I soon lost sight of him. Occasionally I could hear him going through the brush.

Down the canyon a little ways was a draw that went up the hillside to where the cattle were that I had seen. I hoped—and was pretty sure—the bull would go up that draw.

When I finally made my way down off the north to the bottom, I started on down the canyon. Tom had always encouraged us to do a lot of hollering when riding the brushy areas, to stir up the cattle that might be laying in the brush, so every little while I let out a whoop.

This went on for a ways when all of a sudden, not thirty feet ahead of me, there was a crashing and thrashing in the brush. My first thought was, with me doing all that hollerin', I couldn't believe I had actually startled the bull. He had to have known that I was coming. At that moment two bears bolted out of the brush.

Brownie was about thirty feet behind me. Knowing what a hunter he had been, I looked back to see what he would do. He stopped in his tracks then turned his head to the side to watch the bears go up the north. When they were out of sight and we could not hear them anymore, Brownie looked at me and came plodding on down the trail.

When I told Tom that I spooked out a couple of bears he immediately asked, "What did Brownie do?" I told him and he just said, "Darn!" and shook his head. He knew Brownie's tracking days were over. Back when dogs were used to hunt bears and cougars, he had treed many a critter for Tom.

Brownie had a lot of heart. He just wouldn't quit working even when he got up in years and it started getting hard for him to get around. He lived to be sixteen.

Tom and Kelly's wedding day. Me, driving Mattie and Lucie

Tom and Kelly got married in 2008.

As the years passed, Tom's girls, Aspen and Chloe, grew and became more and more help. They developed a real love for the ranch and the work it required. They became good little riders and helped gather cattle. They became big and strong enough to help with the brandings. They pushed calves into the branding chute and they gave shots.

Their background of ranch life gave them solid foundations for very successful experiences in 4-H and FFA. They showed champion steers and other livestock. They excelled in livestock judging and public speaking!

While the girls were maturing into capable young ladies, there were additions to the family in the form of two little boys—Joe and T.J.

Driving down Main St. of Joseph to Thunder Room at the rodeo grounds, for wedding reception

Chloe giving shots

Aspen pushing calves into branding chute

Kelly and T.J.

Chloe and Aspen

Kelly, Joe and Tom

THE HEARING PLACE

When I was a little kid, Fred and Clara Hearing owned the Hearing Place. They had a huge pond, which was stocked with catfish. In fact, there were so many fish that there wasn't enough food for them. They weren't growing; they had big heads and little bodies.

Fred and Clara were friends of my folks. They knew we liked to fish, so they invited us to catch as many fish as we could. One summer we caught close to three hundred fish and ate every one of them! I was so sick of catfish I hoped to never see another catfish the rest of my life!

Recently, when looking at the pond I suspected it was greatly overstocked again. There was no vegetation in the pond!

The Hearing Pond

Tom basically had three different herds: the cattle he ran on the Cougar Creek allotment, the cattle he ran on the Swamp Creek allotment, and the cattle he summered on the Hearing Place. The herds that were run on Cougar Creek and Swamp Creek were branded and earmarked the same. The herd on the Hearing Place was not earmarked and had big tags in their ears so it was easy to identify them. The Hearing cattle were put with the Cougar Creek cattle during the winter—calving season—but the Swamp Creek cattle were never mixed with the Cougar Creek cattle. Cattle did better if they were run on the same range year after year. They learned where the water holes and salt licks were. Also they knew the terrain and where the best grazing was. This was why it was so important that the Cougar Creek cattle and the Swamp Creek cattle were never mixed!

The Hearing Corrals

In the spring, the Swamp Creek calves were branded at the Prairie Creek Place in the valley; the Cougar Creek and Hearing Place calves were branded at the ranch on Crow Creek. Other than this, all working of cattle was done at the Hearing Place.

The Hearing Place was fenced in such a way that five pastures funneled into the corral area, so different herds could be brought in, worked, sorted, and put back out to pasture without ever mixing the herds.

In the fall the three herds were run through the chute to give the cows their fall vaccinations; the calves were given their pre-weaning shots, and later the calves were weaned from their mothers. The larger calves were immediately put on a truck and shipped to feed lots.

Mack ad Marian poling the chute

Lunchtime

Chloe, Kelly and Joe

Tom giving shots

Tom, Aspen and Chloe

One fall Tom sent Ted, Ted's sister, Jane Flanagan, and me to move the Cougar Creek cattle from Crow Creek to the Hearing Place. We had to take them up the Crow Creek Road a ways then push them up a draw to the top. When we got to the top we pushed them to the southeast corner of the pasture. At this corner the cattle had to go out into a pasture where the Swamp Creek cattle were, then out another gate and into a third pasture.

The Swamp Creek cattle heard the cattle we were driving, and came running to see what was going on. The fence between these two herds of cattle was old and low. The cattle could jump it in most places if they really wanted to.

Knowing that it was imperative that these two herds not mix really put the pressure on us. Ted went ahead to open the gates, but couldn't get the Swamp Creek cattle out of the corner. After trying for a while he radioed me for help. I went to help him, but we found that even with both of us we could not drive them away, and down the ridge. They kept turning back and running to the corner. It was like trying to herd flies! We were running our horses to death, and we had no dogs!

Meanwhile the cattle we had brought to the top decided they'd hung around long enough so they turned and tried to go back. Jane had been left alone to keep them in the corner. She radioed for help, but all I could tell her was, "Do the best you can. I can't leave here—the cattle are about to get mixed!"

I guess the cattle finally tired of the "game" because they gave up and we were able to push them down the ridge. I hurried back and helped Jane bring the other cattle through the gates. We were all exhausted by this time, but still had miles to go. At least the hardest part was over. It was one of the most stressful situations I had been in for a long time! I can't even imagine the repercussions of those cattle getting mixed!

I talked with Tom later, encouraging him to do something to distinguish one herd from the other. It was not a matter of IF they would ever mix, but WHEN!

After having several of these horrendous experiences, I knew it was absolutely necessary that I get a couple of stock dogs. I started asking around, but it was hard to find what I wanted—Border Collies that were bred to work. I preferred adult dogs that were ready to go to work. After inquiring for quite some time I finally got a lead. Monica Jennings, who worked in the school cafeteria at Enterprise, told me that her husband, Greg, was needing to get rid of some dogs. They had just given away a year-old female, but they were giving away her litter of puppies. I chose a cute little female that I named Paige. After a few weeks, Monica told me that the man they gave the adult female to had returned her. It seems she couldn't get along with his other dogs. Did I want her? Of course I jumped at the opportunity! Her name was Jo. I started taking Jo with me immediately—the fall gather of 2009—then took Paige as soon as she got old enough—the spring and summer of 2010.

They proved to be a lot of help and were very smart, but because they didn't get to work very often, they never developed to their full potential. To be really good at anything, dogs are like people: they need to do a lot of it!

The Hearing Place was all open country; there were no timbered or brushy canyons. It was on the western edge of the Zumwalt Prairie. Some of the place used to be cultivated so was virtually free of rocks, but the uncultivated hills were rocky with bunch grass.

Most of the time Tom used his ATV when moving cattle on this range. Sometimes he had me on an ATV. Other times he had me ride my horse.

When moving cattle from the ranch on Crow Creek to the Hearing Place, the cattle had to be driven up some steep canyons, which had timbered 'norths,' before reaching the open top. Once we were on top, we traveled cross-country through this open range, passing through a neighbor's pasture.

One time, Tom and I had moved cattle to the Hearing Place. Tom was on an ATV and I was on Chip. The pickup and trailer had been left on the Crow Creek Road, at the mouth of Doe Gulch, so we wouldn't have to

Looking south on Hearing Place. Arrow points to Hearing Corrals.

Wallowa Mountains in the background

ride all the way back to the ranch at the end of the day. When we headed home, Tom, who was on the ATV, went on ahead since he could travel faster than me, on my horse. I didn't want him to have to wait a long time for me when he reached the pickup so I was galloping Chip down the old wagon road that went to a homestead up Doe Gulch.

The guy who owned this property at the time, had the road made wider so he could drive a pickup up the draw. The dirt was cut from the bank and spread across the road, making it wider and smoother. In one place the "new dirt" was quite deep. It had been raining so the dirt had turned to mud and I didn't consider just how deep it could be.

We hit it at a full gallop. Chip's front legs went in about to his knees; he dropped his rear end and pulled his front feet out. Of course we were still going in a forward motion because of the momentum. He stuck his front feet down in the mud again, then a third time, before we came to a stop.

Most horses would have gone "tail over teakettle," tumbling and sending the rider flying off! Because of his extreme athletic ability and smart, quick thinking, again Chip had saved me from injury. We continued on down the canyon, and Tom didn't have to wait very long!

I have to tell you about the homestead mentioned in the last story. It is called The Harl Place, and is located up the south fork of Doe Gulch. The old house is still there. It is nestled in a draw, which has a spring and huge pine trees nearby.

It is said that at one time there was a "still" under the floor of the house. I have probed around in the remains of the old house, but can find no hole in which a still could have been hidden. Of course, it has been a long time since anyone lived in the house, and all kinds of varmints have dug up the ground extensively, so if there was a hole under the floor, it possibly has been filled up with these "diggings."

There are a couple of versions of the following story. The Harl family consisted of Mr. Harl, Mrs. Harl, a son, and possibly some other children. It seems that Mr. Harl regularly came home drunk and he and his son disagreed often.

Here is where the story takes different versions. Some say that Mr. Harl came home drunk one night and started beating Mrs. Harl, as he often did. The son became outraged and shot his father, killing him.

The Harl Place

The Harl Place, front view

Others say that Mrs. Harl died and Mr. Harl brought home a young woman. Whether or not they were married, I don't know. The son showed an interest in this young woman. Whether or not they were fooling around, I don't know, but there was a fight and the son shot his father. The next morning the son rode over the hill to the Zurcher Place and told them what he had done. Mr. Zurcher accompanied him to town where he turned himself in, pleading self-defense. He was acquitted.

Some other homesteaders of the area came by the Harl Place the next day and Mr. Harl's body was still in the ditch by the road, out in front of the house.

This story is completely hearsay and I have no idea how much of it is true. I do know that every time I drive cattle by the place, I recall and ponder the stories.

SWAMP CREEK RANGE

The first few years I rode for Tom, the cattle that were going to summer on the Swamp Creek range were trucked to a log landing at the end of the road on Miller Ridge. The cattle were then driven on down the ridge to Vawter Springs. If Tom hadn't already scattered salt, sometimes I packed it on my mules.

As the years went by, the road became so bad that the trucks could no longer haul the cattle to the top so they were unloaded down on Elk Creek at Danny's Camp and driven to Alford Flat where they were left for the night. Tom got up early the next morning and got to the cattle while they were still bedded down—before they started to scatter. He then trailed them to the log landing and on down Miller Ridge.

The first fall I was riding for Tom, 2003, we were gathering the Swamp Creek range. Tom sent Ted Sahlfeld and me down into Swamp Creek. We were to go down Swamp Creek as far as the meadow just below the cow camp.

At about a quarter of a mile up Swamp Creek from the cow camp, a fence started along the east side of the bottom of the canyon. It continued to the meadow just below the cow camp where it cut across the meadow, going to the west side of the canyon.

We found some cattle on the uphill side of this fence. They took off running down country when they saw us. The only way for us to get ahead of them was to drop into the bottom and try to beat them to the meadow. We had to go at a gallop, crossing the creek a couple of times. We did beat the cattle, with enough time to spare that I could have slowed down before I crossed the creek for the last time, to get on the trail in front of the cows.

I was going at a gallop when I came to a log. I had time to pull Chip up and step over the log, but I remembered how gracefully he had jumped the pile of lumber the day I bought him. I just assumed he would do it again. I misjudged. As Chip went up to jump the log, he jumped off to the side, which threw me off to the side. I was grabbing leather just to stay on. When Chip hit the ground I was hanging off to the side, which spooked him and he jumped off to the side again. This took me off. I hit the ground on a frozen mound. My left side, over my kidney, took the brunt of the fall. It knocked the wind out of me and I lay there for a few moments.

The whole ordeal scared Chip and he ran to Ted and his horse. Ted caught him and brought him back over to me. By this time, I had caught my breath so we remounted and headed up Swamp Creek with the cattle.

By the time the day's ride was completed I was hurting pretty badly, but this was the first day of the ride and I wasn't going to miss the rest of the gather! At that time, I didn't have a camper trailer at Tom's so I had to drive back to my place in the valley each night. I left Chip at the ranch so I wouldn't have to haul him back and forth. Ted helped me by having him saddled each morning. I did finish the gather, but shouldn't have. Riding each day kept the bruised area hemorrhaging. My side hurt more every day—to the point that I would have to grab the steering wheel to pull myself up, to get into the pickup.

Log landing at end of Miller Ridge

Headed toward Vawter Spring from log landing

Packing salt on breaks of Swamp Creek

Headed for Alford Flat

I went back to school the day after the gather ended, but I couldn't make it through the day. The bruise was completely around my left side and the soreness increased with the decrease of motion after quitting riding.

Once in late spring we were pushing cattle into the lower Miller Ridge country. Earlier that spring we had pushed them down the breaks on the Joseph Creek side. Tom was checking the Barney Flat area to see if there were still any cows over there. I was gathering the Miller Ridge area. I had gotten down the ridge to the area where I had ridden Chip on that very first ride with him. Not too far down the ridge past the log landing was a spring-fed pond, almost at the top of the ridge. It was a good place for cattle to gather, and sure enough, I picked up about twenty pairs there. As I approached them, I started hollering so they would start stringing out along the trail. Along this part of the ridge there are places where the ridge top is only several feet wide. It forces the cattle to string out single file. Knowing this, I wanted them to get started rather than bunch up. As a result of my hollering, some of them did start down the trail, even before I got to the pond. Because of this, I

Joseph Creek breaks

didn't get a close look at the lead cattle right then. When we came to a place where the ridge top widened some, the cattle spread out. It was then that I noticed a bull in the bunch. The cattle were in a place where I couldn't get a look at the bull's head; I couldn't see ear tags or earmarks. I thought it was too early for Tom to have bulls in, but thought maybe he had done things differently for some reason. I called him on the radio and told him what I had found.

Well, it wasn't Tom's bull. He was a bull who had breached the fence from a neighboring pasture. He belonged to another guy.

Tom said he would be over to help just as soon as he could. I held the cattle and started to go through the bunch and push the bull out, when I noticed a couple of pairs that also were strays. I was able to cut the bull away from the cows, cut out the stray pairs, and start back up the ridge with them. I knew I would meet Tom somewhere.

Joseph Creek below

When I met Tom he was amazed that I was able to cut the bull away from the herd, especially when I told him he would be having an early calf! He asked me how I had done it. I told him I knew I had help—guardian angels. You see, I pray, even when I am out driving cattle—sometimes it seems it's not *humanly* possible to get it done!

Tom took the stray cattle down Driveway Canyon to near the bottom of Swamp Creek. I went back and pushed my bunch on down Miller Ridge toward Vawter Springs.

It was the spring of 2007 and Tom needed some cattle moved from the Beef Pasture, on the Swamp Creek range, to the Snake Pasture on down the Swamp Creek Canyon. He was tied up with other responsibilities so he asked me if I thought I could do it alone. I told him I could try!

It was the first time Tom had sent me alone on a job of this magnitude; it would be an all-day deal. I had the feeling I needed to tell someone where I was going, so the night before I called a friend, Carolyn Witty. I explained where I was going and what I was going to be doing. I would call her when I got home. If I didn't call, she was to call me to see if I had just forgotten to call her. If she couldn't get ahold of me, she was to call Tom. Because Tom and I would be working miles apart, he might not be able to check to see if I made it out and how my day went.

It was in June, thus the days could be getting quite warm down in the canyon, so I decided that I needed to get an early start. I left my place in the valley, drove out the North Highway, took the Charlais Road (Wellamotkin Drive), went up over Starvation Ridge, down into Swamp Creek, and up the other side to the top of Miller Ridge. I then dropped down into Elk Creek and went down it to as far as Danny's Camp. Danny's Camp is about a mile and a half up Elk Creek from Tom's house on Crow Creek. At Danny's Camp, a canyon with an old logging road in it, takes off to the north-northwest, eventually topping out on Miller Ridge.

I took this road and topped out on Miller Ridge, at about where the Chico Trail comes up out of Swamp Creek. I parked, unloaded Chip, and was in the saddle a little before 6:00 a.m. I rode through the gate into the Beef Pasture, which extends from the breaks—the edges of hilltops or ridges where it starts down into the canyon—down to the bottom of Swamp Creek. Tom had said the cattle were hanging along the top and down into the breaks a ways. I rode the top and the breaks. I didn't have any dogs at that time so it was a pretty slow process. I pushed the cattle north along the top until I reached the head of Nell's Canyon. When I tried to get the cows to go down the ridge and drop into Nell's Canyon, it was like pushing a chain! Poor ol' Chip! It was back and forth, back and forth. Then even when I did get them started down the bottom of Nell's Canyon, they wouldn't stay in the bottom, but graded out onto one hillside then the other.

Blanche Maxwell and Carolyn Witty coming out of Swamp Creek Cow Camp, Nell's Canyon in background

It was 3:00 p.m. by the time I got to the bottom of Swamp Creek. I stopped for about fifteen minutes to inhale a sandwich and let Chip drink and rest. I noticed a bloody spot on Chips left front foot, right at the hairline above the hoof. It wasn't bleeding much and he wasn't limping so I didn't think much of it.

I was supposed to push the cattle down Swamp Creek, through the gate, and into the Snake Pasture. If I quit before I put them through the gate and closed it, everything I had done all that day would be for naught. The cattle would go right back to where they had come from!

The bottom of the Swamp Creek Canyon was fenced off. It was a riparian zone that cattle were not supposed to graze. This fence kept the cattle from getting into the very bottom and all the brush, and kept them up on the hillside a little ways, in most places. When the trail was going along a dry, rocky hillside where there wasn't much to eat, the cattle went relatively well, but each time we came to the mouth of a draw where there was better soil depth and lush green grass, they would completely stop. They were hungry after having been driven for so many hours. I did finally get them through the gate. I could tell Chip was exhausted and we still had to climb to the top of Miller Ridge. My plan was to go back up Swamp Creek to the mouth of Miller Canyon then go up it to the top.

Even though the days were long, I was afraid we were going to run out of daylight. Miller Canyon had been burned out years ago. As in most burned canyons, the brush had grown back so thickly that in some places a horse could hardly push his way through it. When pushing through it, the horse couldn't see the trail—see where to put his feet. In many places old burned trees had fallen across the trail—some so big there was no way to get across them. In some places it took several attempts before finding a way through. Chip usually had a gait of slow and steady when climbing up a draw such as this. He seldom asked to stop, but this night he kept stopping. I felt bad for the poor old guy—I knew he was exhausted so I let him stop and rest as much as I dared. I knew we absolutely had to make it to the top before it was completely dark. We did finally reach the top. The rest of the way back to the rig would be basically flat, except for a few "ups" and "downs" as the road made its way along the ridge top. I knew we would make it just fine, even with just starlight, once we reached the top.

We got back to the rig a little after 10:00 p.m. I loaded up and started the slow, rough, crooked descent back down to Elk Creek. When I got to Danny's Camp I started up the Elk Creek road. I had made it to the top of Miller's Ridge, dropped down into Swamp Creek, and was headed up the other side when I saw headlights coming toward me. My first thought was, "Why in the world is someone coming into this country at this time of night?" It was almost 11:00 p.m. by that time. My next thought was, "Do you suppose someone ... ?"

I slowed down as the rig approached me. It had slowed down too. As we passed each other, in the reflection of our lights, I could see it was a flatbed pickup with an ATV. In my mirror I could see him hit his brakes; I hit mine. With me pulling a trailer, it was easier for him to back up than me. We both rolled down our windows and there was Cory Miller. The first thing he said was, "Julie, are you okay?" When I got home I discovered that I had dried blood on my face, apparently from going through the brush. Next, Cory asked what had happened. I told him it had turned into a horrendous day, being by myself and with no dogs! Yes, Cory was coming out to look for me! Tom had called him. When I met Cory he was able to make contact with Tom, and the whole "search-for-Julie plan" that Tom had put in place was aborted.

The next morning Chip couldn't even set his foot down. He had a bad bruise along the coronary band of the foot. I wasn't able to ride him for weeks. When his hoof started growing out, the hoof was deformed where the injury had been. As it grew out it continued to get worse. His hoof ended up having a crack from the hairline to the tip of his hoof. I credited my farrier, Ted Freels, with saving that hoof. Ted made a barred shoe for that foot; he filled the crack with J B Weld; he rasped off the rough, deformed growth on the hoof. Chip had to have this special care for years, but that foot stayed sound and I continued to ride him after that first few weeks of healing.

The next time I saw Tom, the story unfolded of what had happened on his end that night. Carolyn had called Tom to tell him that I had not made it out. Tom told her he knew that, and assured her that he was "on it" and for her not to worry. He knew where I was going to leave my rig so in the evening he went up to check to see if I had made it out. I hadn't: my rig was still there. He went back to the ranch to give me more time then he went up again to check on me. I still wasn't out of the canyon.

This time when he reached the bottom, at Danny's Camp, he took the bough of an evergreen tree and "swept" the road to rid it of any tracks. He then went back to the ranch and called his mom, Marian, to come and stay with the girls so he could go looking for me. He also called Kelly, his girlfriend at the time—later they were married—to go with him. Tom and Kelly were going to hike, retracing my route along the top and down Nell's Canyon. He contacted Cory Miller and Cory was to go down the bottom of Swamp Creek on his ATV to the cow camp. They thought that if I was hurt I might hole up in the old cabin at the cow camp. Rod Childers was going to go out North Highway 3 and get out on a ridge so they could contact him from the bottom of the canyon. Rod would then relay the message if any further help was needed. When I was talking to Tom he said, "You know Julie, if you had been hurt, we would have found you. We would have found you!" I have absolutely no doubt that they would have.

Dave Caudle on Cricket

That fall of 2007, a friend of mine, Dave Caudle from Peachland, B.C., Canada, came down and rode a few days with me when we did the fall gather on the Swamp Creek allotment.

I borrowed, Carolyn Witty's horse, Cricket, for Dave to ride. Tom sent us out to the log landing on Miller Ridge. We took the trail down Driveway Canyon to the bottom Swamp Creek, up Swamp Creek past the old cow camp a ways, then took a draw to the top of Miller Ridge. Later, we pushed the cows down into Elk Creek, up the other side to Fire Ridge, into the Dorrance Pasture, then on to the Catch Fly Pasture to be sorted.

COUGAR CREEK RANGE

In the spring we put the cattle that were going to summer on the Cougar Creek range up Sumac one year and up Trap Canyon the next year. When we went to Trap Canyon we drove them down the Joseph Creek Road. The challenge was keeping them from mixing with Bob Lathrop's cattle as we passed through.

At the mouth of Trap Canyon there was a high steep bank that the cattle had to climb. We scattered a little hay up this bank to get them started. By the time they got to the top they were winded. It was hard to get them to move on up through the gate. After we did get them through the gate we let them rest and mother-up. Once the cows had found their babies they started trailing on up the canyon.

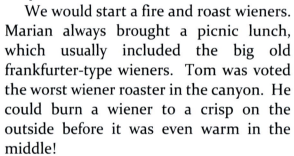

Tom, Marian, Kelly, Bud, and Mack

Tom roasting a wiener

We would start a fire and roast wieners. Marian always brought a picnic lunch, which usually included the big old frankfurter-type wieners. Tom was voted the worst wiener roaster in the canyon. He could burn a wiener to a crisp on the outside before it was even warm in the middle!

After we gave the cattle a while to trail up the canyon, a couple of us started up after them. We pushed them up to the forks where we let them stop. Many times Tom would then have me stay with the cattle for a couple more hours, until they were all mothered up. I left my rig at the mouth of Trap Canyon, so when the cows were all mothered up, I rode back down the canyon, loaded my horse, and drove back to the ranch.

North Fork of Trap Canyon

Letting cattle "mother-up"

Tom generally had already taken salt up. If he hadn't, he had me balance a block on my saddle horn and take it up as we were pushing the cows. The only time it was difficult was when I was going through the brush. It took one hand to rein Chip, one hand to balance the salt, and that left no hand to push the brush aside, out of my face. When Tom salted from out on top, there were some places he couldn't go with the ATV, so occasionally we packed salt on my mules.

Me, packing salt into Trap Canyon

'Souths' were bare, but 'norths' had snow

Making plans for the day's ride

The fall gathers on both the Swamp Creek range and the Cougar Creek range were usually done in the last half of October. A good share of the time the weather was mild and we rode in shirtsleeves, but other times it was cold and snowy. It was a "catch-22" situation because if the weather was mild it made for a more pleasant gather, but at the same time it made it more difficult to gather the cattle, because they weren't ready to go home!

When there was snow on the ground it would ball up on the horses' feet so they had no traction and were much more apt to lose their footing. When the trees were full of snow, the snow dumped down our necks and filled our laps to the point I at times could not even see my saddle horn. I have scooped it out just to have my saddle full again after going another twenty-to-thirty feet through the timber!

The Cougar Creek Basin was a complex of many steep canyons and ridges. The "souths" were rocky, but covered with bunch grass. The norths were even steeper than the souths. They were covered with thick timber and brush, to the extent that they were virtually

Ted Sahlfeld and I bringing cattle off Sleepy Bill

impassable except for a few places where old logging roads graded through them, connecting the canyon bottoms with the ridge tops.

In some places there were open points—places where there were no trees or brush—going off of these roads. Occasionally cattle would grade around a road then out onto one of these points. They would sometimes even grade around through the timbered north.

It could be very difficult to get cattle out of these norths. The riders usually rode the logging roads, most of which had been overgrown with timber and brush, but at least they were flat enough to ride a horse around. If cattle were spotted in a place where a horse couldn't go, dogs were sent in after them. If a rider didn't have dogs, he would have to tie his horse to a tree and go afoot. Sometimes the cattle would start moving as the result of a lot of yelling and whistling.

The biggest challenge was spotting the cattle. When possible, a rider was sent along the south, across the canyon from the north. This rider could then look into the north and see cattle, which the rider in the north couldn't see. If something were spotted, the rider on the south would radio the rider in the north with the information. The rider in the north could at the same time be looking for cattle on the south that might be out of sight from that rider.

One time, Tom, Doug McDaniel, and I were riding the main fork of the Cougar Creek Basin. Tom sent me around one of the logging roads. He and Doug were going to go around the face of the south across the canyon from me. The south was so steep that they were leading their horses. They were looking for cattle in my north, and I was looking for cattle on their south.

When Tom came on the radio, after his first few words, I knew there was trouble. He said, "Oh, Julie, I am so sorry to have to ask you to do this, but you are the only rider in that area. There are some cows above the road you are on, and about 300 yards ahead of you."

I didn't have dogs at that time so would have to get them by going horseback. Tom said he would watch me and tell me when I needed to get above the road. This north was so steep that the banks of the road, both the uphill side and the downhill side, were so steep you couldn't get a horse off the road. In a few places the road cut through a swale, thus there was no bank on the uphill side.

After I had gone a ways Tom radioed me and said I should probably try to get above the road at the next swale. The swale was full of brush, but Chip pushed his way through it. Chip then had to dig and claw his way up the hillside to where we would be at the level of the cattle. When I unsaddled that night I found that the breast collar had rubbed a sore on Chip's chest. That is how hard a climb it was!

I graded around to where the cattle were. At the same time, I saw Jerry Winegar coming toward me on the road I had been on originally. He had been coming down the ridge at the top of the north I was on, so when he heard Tom, he came to help me.

The cattle would grade around through the north until they came to the open ridge Jerry had just come down. Jerry hollered at me and told me to try to get ahead of them and turn them down the ridge. He didn't want them to go up the ridge.

There was no trail where I was so I couldn't make very good time. I hurried Chip along as fast as I dared when I came to where a huge pine tree had fallen up the hill. It had left a hole in the ground where the roots were pulled up and the roots were sticking out over the hole. There was another pine tree, still standing, right next to the hole.

I knew I had to hurry, and it would take extra time to go down around the standing tree. I had to make a quick decision of what to do. Should I go around or try to make it between the roots and the standing tree? I saw one root in particular that was sticking out over the hole quite a ways. I knew if we got caught up on anything it would be that root. It didn't look to be too big so I thought that if we did hook on it, it would break off or at least bend. All of these thoughts went through my mind in a split second. The one thing I neglected to consider was just how hard and strong these pine roots were.

Chip entered the space between the root and the tree, and when the root did hook up on my saddle or Chip's shoulder—I'm not sure which—Chip pushed forward with all his might, but the root did not break. It bent forward a little then sprang back, pushing Chip backwards. As Chip went backwards, the rein on the uphill side hooked on a root. This jerked on Chip's mouth, turning his head uphill and at the same time his rear end downhill. The jerk on his bit caused him to rear.

As he was rearing, I remember thinking, "I'm going to go just like Lee did!" As he reared I could hear and feel Chip shuffling his hind feet downhill, trying to save himself from going over backwards. At the same time, he swung the front of his body sideways so when his front feet hit the ground he was standing parallel with the hillside, then he just stopped. He stood perfectly still, seeming to not be the least bit upset.

It was then that I noticed that the rein that had caught on the root was broken right where it attaches to the bit. If Chip had thrown a fit, I would have had to bail off as I had no control of him with just one rein. I quickly dismounted on the uphill side, ran the rein through the loop on the shank of the bit, and tied it.

Ted, Tom, Kelly and Doug McDaniel

Jerry had been busy trying to find a place where he could go up the bank, to get above the road, so hadn't seen what had happened with Chip and me. When he saw me off my horse he asked if I was okay. I said I was, but had a broken rein. He asked if I was going to be able to get ahead of the cattle. I said I would be on my way in just a minute. I mounted and this time I went down around the tree. I hurried on around the north and got out onto the ridge, then headed the cattle down country. Jerry and I took the cattle on down to the bottom of Cougar Creek where we met up with the rest of the riders. We stopped for lunch, and of course Doug built a fire. Doug always built a fire!

While eating our lunches I told the guys that I had a broken rein. I was concerned because we still had to go through several more norths then up some canyons and ridges before we topped out up on Red Hill. Dave Yost rode with us that day. He carried a Leatherman and some leather shoestring so he repaired my broken rein.

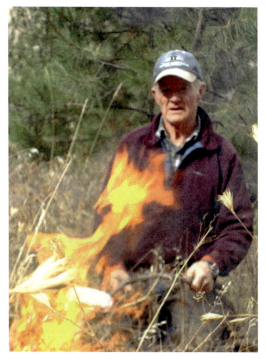

Doug always built a fire.

At the end of the day

    The summer of 2015 was exceptionally dry. Water was scarce, grass was short, and cattle had to be moved often. It was July 2nd and Tom wanted to move cattle out of Sumac and put them in the lower end of Cougar Creek. Tom wanted to get an early start so we could finish before it got really hot! I got up at 4:00 a.m. and headed for Crow Creek. I met up with Tom and got my instructions for the ride. I was to trailer to the top. Tom was going up Sumac on the ATV with his three dogs. I trailered to the top of Red Hill then out a logging road to a gravel pit on the breaks of Sumac.

    As I rode down the point I could see about ten pairs scattered all over the hillside on the north side of Denny Gulch. Way down on the point I was riding, I found two pairs. I left them alone and went on to check in a swale next to the fence to see if any critters were over there. There weren't.

    Even though I had not disturbed the first two pairs, they must have been stirred up by the sight of my dogs because by the time I got back to where I had first seen them, they were gone! I just caught sight of the tail ends of them as they dove off into the north.

    The plan had been to take them around an old logging road that graded into the bottom of Denny Gulch, then go down Denny picking up anything I might find along the way. I would push the cattle down to the bottom of Sumac. Tom was going to come up Sumac, picking up anything that might be in the bottom then push them up to the mouth of Denny. He would wait there, and turn my cattle up Sumac where his cattle would have gone. As happened so often, the cattle had a way of changing our plans. Thank goodness we had radios so we could keep each other informed of what was going on!

    The two pairs I had picked up on the point, dove off into the north, alright, but then did not drop down to the logging road. They stayed above it, side-hilling around through the brush and downed timber until they came to a swale. At that point, rather than drop down to the road, they headed up the swale on a trail that led to a pond that was dry. They shot past the pond and out onto the open ridge that I had come down not long ago, then they headed up the ridge to where I had left my pickup and trailer.

Tom had said that if I found a couple of pairs way off from any other cattle, and close to a gate, I was to put them through the gate. The adjoining pasture would be ridden in the near future anyway. By the time I caught up with the cattle they were almost to the gate by my pickup so I opened it and let them through.

Since I had just ridden the ridge, I decided to drop into Denny by going down the fence line, rather than going down the ridge again. The trails that followed a fence into the bottom were usually quite steep because the fences went straight down the norths.

Pushing cattle down Cunningham Ridge

I hit the bottom and rode down Denny, to where Tom was waiting, without finding any cattle. I decided that I needed to go back up the point north of Denny and get the cattle I had seen earlier. They had graded around into the north so I put the dogs on them, which pushed them to the bottom of the next canyon, East Sumac. I rode on up the ridge to the fence line then took a trail along the fence to the bottom of East Sumac and started down the canyon, picking up cattle as I went.

Earlier Tom had radioed and said he would come up East Sumac and turn the cattle up the Bill Fine Salt Trough Trail. As I was going down the canyon, Tom called again and said he had spotted some cattle on Cunningham Ridge and was going after them, so he wouldn't be there to turn my cattle. I was just to do the best I could.

It was getting hotter as the day went on. There was no water for my dogs in most places. They were getting hot, so were not working very well for me. As I went down the canyon I was trying to form a plan to get ahead of the cattle. The canyon was narrow and brushy so I couldn't just slip by them. This was when good "heading" dogs would have been worth their weight in gold!

The canyon widened a little right where the Bill Fine Trail took off up a draw and there was a brushy spot off the trail. The cattle pulled off into the brush; they were getting hot too. I was able to get ahead and turn the cattle, but rather than go up the Bill Fine Trail, they headed back up the canyon we had just come down. I was able to get ahead of about half of them and start them up the right trail. My dogs helped me get ahead of the rest of the cows. As I pushed them back down the canyon they saw the other cows headed up the Bill Fine Trail so they followed.

Right away one old cow let me know she did not have her calf. She kept bawling and trying to go back. I was hoping her calf was up on the ridge where we were headed—that she had gone in for water and left it behind. We went on up the ridge almost to the fence when I saw some cattle up ahead. The cow was still bawling, and sure enough, a calf from up ahead started answering her. They were a pair!

Tom radioed and said he had gotten the cattle off Cunningham Ridge and had pushed them through the gate, so he would be right over to help me. When he got to me he said he and the dogs could take the cattle on from there.

At this point I was several miles from my rig, but it was only 11:00 a.m. so he wanted me to ride back to my rig, load up and trailer down to Crow Creek and gather a pasture down there. He would come and help me as soon as he pushed these cattle through the gate. When I got to my rig it was 90 degrees.

It took quite a while to ride back to my rig and trailer off Red Hill and up Crow Creek to where I was supposed to start riding. Tom was on the ATV, so when he got the cows through the gate he zipped right along, came down Sumac, and was to the pasture up Crow Creek within minutes of my getting there.

We were going to push cattle that were hanging along the bottom of Crow Creek up Culvert Canyon. As we got the cattle out of the brush at the mouth of the canyon, Tom made a passing comment that he hoped there were no more in the brush up along the creek. It was so brushy up along the creek a horse couldn't be ridden along it without a lot of effort and time. He sure couldn't take the ATV!

We gathered up the cattle and started them up the canyon. When I had ridden that canyon the previous fall I discovered that there were some fallen trees across the trail that made it impossible to ride a horse up the bottom. I told Tom, so he had thrown a chain saw on the ATV. He cut out the trees and I proceeded up the canyon. The canyon was shaded most of the way, thus it was not quite so hot for the cattle.

Tom took the ATV around another way and planned to meet me on top. I picked up more cattle as I went along and Tom found some on top. We put them together then pushed them out the gate into another pasture. Tom counted them out and found that we were short a bull.

I had to ride back to my rig the way I had come. Tom went another way and headed for the ranch. He was going to gather up some fencing material and tools, and go to the Hearing Place and fix fence. I was going to load up and head back to the valley. When I got back down to the mouth of Culvert Canyon and was letting my horse get a drink out of Crow Creek, I looked in the brush and there he was—the missing bull.

By this time it was getting late in the afternoon and getting hotter by the hour, but I knew I couldn't leave the bull. He would wander off and we would have to ride the entire pasture just to find one bull! I decided the best thing to do was put him in the road and take him to the ranch. Tom could then haul the bull to where ever he wanted him.

We had left the gate into the road open so I could go out it when I got back down out of the canyon. I started easing the bull toward the gate, but he blew past me and dove off into the creek and brush. I got him out and once more tried to ease him toward the gate. Once again he bolted past me, crossed the creek and started up along the creek. I went up on the hillside into the timber, since the brush right along the creek was too thick to ride through, and got ahead of the bull. I drove him back down to the creek where he stood in the middle of it, in some brush where I couldn't ride. I backed off a ways then came at him very fast, screaming and yelling as loud as I could. I guess I bluffed the ol' boy because he climbed the bank on the other side and started along the fence. This gave me time to find a gap in the brush so I could cross and get in behind him.

The problem was that the gate was in a swale so the bull couldn't see it until he got right to it. I got him to the swale, but he still didn't see the gate. Instead, he headed down toward the creek, so I headed him back up the swale and he finally saw the gate!

I headed him down the road then went back to my rig, jumped my horse in the trailer, turned around, and started following the bull down the road as I drove my rig along. I assumed Tom was long gone to the Hearing Place, but as I came around a corner, there was Tom. He helped me put the bull in the Elk Creek pasture with some cows. Tom then headed on to the Hearing Place and I decided that since I was at Elk Creek I might as well go home by way of the Charlais Road/North Highway. The thermometer in my pickup said 101 degrees. So much for getting an early start so we could quit before it got too hot!

It was August and time to move the cattle out of Cougar Creek—the cattle Tom and I had moved into Cougar a month earlier. Tom called and asked if I could ride later in the week. He would open the gates into the Baldwin Pasture and let the cattle start drifting through, and he would go down Joseph Creek and up the bottom of Cougar Creek as far as he could go on the ATV. He would take the dogs and push the cattle out of the bottom and get them started to the top.

Tom told me to contact Mike Williams to make plans for the ride. I did and Mike said I might as well ride out with him. I was to be at his place in the valley at a little after 5:00 a.m. When I got there he said that Adele Nash was also going to be going with us. When Adele arrived we headed for the Chesnimnus Bridge where we met Jill Yost Hite and her crew. They would be riding for Jill's dad, James Yost. Jill brought her daughter, Emma and a hired man, Jeb Pokorny. Jill would be on an ATV with Emma, and Jeb on horseback.

After a few minutes of making plans for the day we headed up the Red Hill Grade. We trailered to the Huckleberry Corner where we unloaded and started our ride. Mike and I rode the ridges and breaks, as we knew where the water holes were located. We pushed the cattle up to the Cougar Creek Breaks Road that wound around the heads of all the draws and canyons that make up the Cougar Creek Basin. Jeb then pushed them farther up toward the top.

Adele picked up cattle we pushed up to this road, and rode the area between this road and the main Red Hill Road, Forest Service Road #46. Emma stayed on or near the 46 road and pushed cattle north toward our destination. Jill kept going back over the logging roads, checking for cattle that might have been missed. When she found cattle, if they were in such a place she couldn't get to them on the ATV, she radioed Mike or me and we went back for them. She covered many miles and saved us a lot of back riding. Mike and I had each pushed several bunches to the top where they were picked up by the gals and Jeb.

By watching the sky, we could see that a thunderstorm was building. We had taken slickers so were prepared for a shower. We also had radios so we could keep in touch. I had just headed down toward Aspen, a ridge of the Cougar Creek Basin, when I came upon two bulls. They took off through the timber. I knew I had to keep right on them or they would brush up somewhere and we would miss them. I was able to keep them in sight, so trailed them up to the 46 road and put them with some cattle the gals were driving.

I was headed back down Aspen and Mike was going down Telephone when he radioed me and said, "It looks like we are going to get rained on!" Some threatening clouds were coming at us from the southwest. I flippantly replied, "Yeah, that's why I have my slicker! Ha ha!" I rode on down the ridge. It was amazing how fast that storm built! In just a few minutes the cloud went from a cloud that looked like it was full of moisture to a cloud that was definitely full of *energy*—probably electricity! I quickly untied my slicker from my saddle and slipped it on. I noticed two calves under a big lone pine tree on the ridge top and two cows down on the south hillside. When the cows saw me and my dogs, they started up the hill to their calves.

Cut-out on Bonar Flat

Aspen was a ridge that had a deep saddle—a dip in the ridge—with a rocky point on each side of the saddle. Out on the point, on my side of the saddle, there were four more pairs. I knew it was very dangerous to have cattle under a lone pine, but I also knew if I got them out from under the tree they would more than likely take off into the timber and I would lose them while I went on to get the cattle off the point.

Me, on the left, looking for pairs   Photo by Kelly Birkmaier

The energy in that cloud was building by the moment. I knew it was going to break loose soon. I prayed, "God protect these cattle while I go after the others!" I hurried on to get the cattle off the point. I figured that the lightning would more than likely strike one of the rocky points if it didn't strike the tree. I had just reached the rocky point where the cows were when the lightning struck. It didn't strike the tree, and it didn't strike either rocky point. It struck in the very bottom of that deep saddle! It was as though God was showing me that He could put that lightning wherever He chose! I thanked God for my safety. After the lightning struck, it immediately began to pour, thus there was no fire. As I drove the cattle up the ridge, I had not gone a quarter of a mile when I realized that it hadn't rained at this spot—the trail was dusty! I took my slicker off and was tying it behind my saddle when Chip gave a big jump! I had laid the reins over the saddle horn, so I turned quickly and grabbed for the reins. After a step or two, Chip stopped and started rubbing his face and nose on his foreleg. The cattle had stirred up a bee's nest. I don't know if the bee was on his face or on his leg, but he sure was trying to rub it off! When Chip jumped I could have gone off backwards and broken my neck. This was twice that God had spared my life in less than half an hour. It just reaffirmed what I believe: that each of us have an appointed time—and that day was not my time!

BULLS

I chose to combine most of the "bull stories" to form a chapter just about the "adventures" of dealing with bulls. Bulls can be, and usually are, the challenge of the gather. Bulls seem to have the uncanny ability to know when it is gathering time. They will separate themselves from the cows, go off in a "hole" and hide, or so it seems.

One of the fundamental rules of a gather is: Stay with the bull. If it comes to a choice of bringing in a herd of cows or a lone bull, bring in the bull! A lot of times the cows will keep trailing in once they have a good start, especially if you have gotten them to a main trail or road. Not a bull! He will dive off into the brush when he is in sight of the gate, if given the chance.

When cows won't move, the dogs can generally persuade them to do so. Not a bull! Usually putting the dogs on him will cause him to get on the fight or just "sull-up" (get sullen) and refuse to move.

When climbing out of a canyon you have to give a bull a lot of time. When he wants to stop and rest, you let him rest. If you don't, he will get too hot and tired and will refuse to move, or he will break back past you and head down country to where you just came from.

You have to let the bull think he is the boss, and you have to have patience, patience, and more patience! These strategies work the vast majority of the time, but then there are those exceptions, which I will talk about later.

Both the Swamp Creek range and the Cougar Creek range had heavily brushed and timbered areas. No matter how good a rider you are, occasionally cattle are going to be missed. It just happens.

Because of this, re-rides were automatically scheduled into the gather. After riding an area, many times we would immediately re-ride it, going the opposite direction, as we rode back to our rigs. If the first ride covered such a large area that there wasn't time to re-ride it again that day, we would re-ride it the next day.

One time when we were riding on the Cougar Creek range, Tom told Ted and me to ride back through an area that had just been ridden. We split up so we could cover more area. Sure enough, I soon found a pair. I called on the radio and some other riders came and got the pair so I could go on and help Ted.

Ted had called and said he jumped three bulls and they took off to the bottom of a draw where there was a water hole. He was concerned that if he tried to move them by himself they might get away. We decided he should sit tight until I could get there to help. The trouble was I didn't know exactly where he was. I asked him, over the radio, what he had done, which way he had gone, after we split up. He told me and also described his surrounding, so then I had a pretty good idea of the general area he was in. My goal was to get close enough to him to be able to hear him give a "whoop." I finally got close enough to hear a faint whoop, so had him keep hollering until I could get to where he was. We were able to get the bulls out of the draw.

Once when I was re-riding on the Cougar Creek range I found a bull brushed up and happy to be there. I got him out of the thick brush and started moving along slowly, but it was obvious he didn't want to move. He stopped every little while and scratched his head on a small pine tree. I was trying to keep the balance of making him move yet not rushing him. All of a sudden he whirled around and came at my horse. Chip whirled to the side to keep from getting hit. Sometimes a horse will jump out from under a rider when this happens!

I could see the bull meant business. I also knew there were other riders out there, maybe even close by, who could come and help me. I called Tom on the radio and told him the bull had just taken my horse. I also told him where I was. As I talked on the radio, other riders heard me. In minutes Dave Yost and Chris Daggett were there to help me. We joined forces thinking we could persuade the bull to move.

After the bull took the guys' horses a few times we decided we needed a new plan. I looked at Chris and saw he was taking the shells out of the pistol he was carrying. He was replacing the shells with birdshot. I knew what was coming. Chris shot the bull in the shoulder when he tried to take his horse. The bull kept wanting to take us, so had to be shot several more times. After the third or fourth shot the bull headed down the road like a "club calf" being led. The orneriness was all gone out of him.

Ted and I had brought a bull out of the breaks of Cougar Creek. We needed to get him south of the fence separating the Cougar Creek pasture from the Muddy Reservoir pasture. Even though he was traveling pretty well, I knew we couldn't relax until he was through the gate. I rode on ahead and saw there were some cows on the other side of the fence. I was so intent on getting the bull with the cows I didn't pay any attention to where we were. As soon as we got him through the gate and I had closed it, I looked around and saw my error.

The cows I had seen were also in a wrong pasture. They needed to be in the next pasture to the east. We decided we would gather up the cows, put the bull with them then take all of them to the correct pasture. Ted started after the cows and I went for the bull. When the bull saw me coming, he took off down Sumac like the devil was after him! While I was still in radio range I called Ted and told him I would take the bull to the mouth of Sumac, which was four or five miles away. I would put him in a corral there that was owned by my ex-husband. Ted went on to where the other riders were. Tom quizzed Ted as to where I was and what I was doing. Later Ted told me he told Tom, "The last time I saw her she was after the bull, going through the timber so fast her horse's tail was straight out behind him!" I'm sure that was a slight exaggeration, but I *was* speeding right along. Tom was concerned that I would not be able to get the bull to the corral—it was several miles and I had to go through three gates.

I did make it. When I got to the corral there were some cattle in the pasture that surrounded the corral. While I was getting the corral gate open the bull got with the cattle. I cut the bull from the cows, took him to the corral, put him in, and shut the gate. I looked the corral over to see if I needed to fix anything to assure it would hold the bull. I had, years before, helped my husband build the corral, so I knew how old it was.

The corral was close to two miles from Tom's house. All the way down Sumac I was thinking, "I sure hope someone brings my rig to Sumac so I don't have to ride all the way to Tom's house." They didn't, so I started up the Joseph Creek road toward Tom's house. I had just crossed the Chesnimnus Bridge when Jane came on the radio.

"Julie, do you have a copy?"

"Yes Jane, go ahead," I answered.

"Where are you?"

"I'm between the Chesnimnus Bridge and Tom's house."

Jane then went on to tell me how worried she had been. She could just see me laid out somewhere up Sumac!

Tom had sent Jane on ahead in a rig and she was to keep trying to contact me on the radio as she came off Red Hill and down the Red Hill Grade. When she was able to contact me, she was still high enough on Red Hill to be able to contact Tom and tell him I was okay.

When everyone got down off of Red Hill, we took a pickup and trailer down to the corral to get the bull. By this time, it was dark and Tom was worried that the bull could have broken out and would be gone. He wasn't gone. He loaded up without much trouble, so Tom gave a sigh of relief. One more bull had been captured!

Down Elk Creek a little ways from Danny's Camp was the mouth of a draw that ran about due south. It topped out up on the north end of Fire Ridge.

When driving up Elk Creek we could see part of the open hillside on the west side of the draw. As we were trailering up Elk Creek early one morning, to meet up with the rest of the riders, we spotted three bulls out on this open hillside.

We went on up Elk Creek and met up with everyone and made plans for the day's ride. Tom told me to ride the old skid road that went around through the north above Danny's Camp. I would be able to get out on the point above where we had seen the bulls, and could work my way down the point to where I would be below them.

The bulls paid little attention to me as I approached. I eased up on them and they turned and headed for the trail along the fence that ran up the bottom of the draw for a ways then it pulled up out of the bottom and went diagonally along the hillside. As we went up the fence line we were still headed up the draw, but at the same time were forced to climb higher and higher on the hillside. This was one of those times when I thought I was doing everything right, at least I sure was trying to, and it still didn't work!

Younger, lighter-weight bulls usually were more willing to make a climb. These were older, heavier bulls, so I knew I would have to give them a lot of time. As we eased along the fence, they would go a little way then stop, go a little way and stop. I was letting them do this when all of a sudden they blew past me, going down the hill faster than you would have ever thought possible, considering how steep it was.

I was sitting there on Chip, watching them go, when all of a sudden they stopped as quickly as they had started. They started grazing as though nothing had happened. I sat there for a few moments trying to decide what to do. I decided I had to give it one more try before resigning to the fact that I was whipped.

The bulls were still close enough to the fence and trail that I couldn't go down it or I would cause them to go farther down the draw. I decided to "side hill" around above them then zigzag down the hillside until I was below them. As I was going around the hill I said, "Lord, I'm going to need a little help here." Then I chuckled to myself and said, "No, Lord, I'm going to need a LOT of help."

I did get below them and once again started easing them over toward the trail and fence. It took a lot of time with many rests, but I got them to the top and they didn't once try to go back again.

In the fall of 2015 when I was riding for the Birkmaier Ranch, we had completed the gathering of the Cougar Creek allotment, but knew we were missing some cattle. Tom sent Ted and me to the top to see if we could find anything.

Knowing where the water holes were, and likely places the cattle might be, we started checking them out. We went down to the Gravel Pit Pond. It was just before the opening of elk season and some Indians were camped at the pond. They always came and did their hunting just prior to the opening of elk season. They told us that they had seen some cattle on toward Coyote Camp Ground so we headed that direction. We went clear to Coyote without spotting anything.

As we were on our way back, we hadn't gotten to the Red Hill Lookout when I spotted something in the brush under the road. Ted backed the rig up to where we could see the critter, hoping we would see more than one. We unloaded and went down after the critter, which turned out to be a lone bull—a bull belonging to Mike Williams, another permittee. We got him up on the road then Ted loaded his horse and went to some other places, looking for cattle, as I started down the road with the bull.

The bull went fine for a ways then stopped to scratch on a tree. When he was through scratching, he just stood there. I moved toward him and he still just stood there so I moved closer. He whirled and came at my horse. Ozzie jumped sidewise and scooted out of the way to keep from getting hit. Some bulls will give one big jump toward you then stop and shake their head at you. Not this guy! He kept coming for twenty or thirty feet.

There was an old pine tree nearby which had several dead limbs low enough that I could reach them since I was on my horse. I broke off a big dead limb and threw it at the bull. He turned and headed down the road again. This behavior continued for the next couple of miles. It got to where I just had to shake a limb at him and he would turn and start down the road again.

After checking all the places he could think of, and not finding any more critters, Ted came back to see how I was doing. I was making progress, but I was also burning a lot of daylight. It was mid-October and the days were getting pretty short. It wouldn't be long before dark set in. I was riding my new horse, Ozzie, that I could shoot a gun off of. All this time I was wishing I had a pistol with birdshot in it.

There were two things that were in my favor. It was full moon, and the top of the ridge had only sparse timber in most places, so even when the bull got off the road I still was able to see him. I had to keep that delicate balance of being close enough to the bull to be able to see him—he was a black angus—and not so close that he would come at me. If there had been dense timber and brush for him to dive into I would have had to go off and leave him—I couldn't have gone in after him. He would have "gotten me."

Ted had to keep way back from me because when he got close, the bull turned to see what was coming, and Ozzie kept wanting to turn back to go to Ted's horse in the trailer. Even when Ted turned the lights off, they could hear the rig and it caused trouble. Ted had no way of knowing how far he was behind me until he got close enough to see me, then it was too close, so I would listen for the rig. I would then radio him and say, "That's probably close enough."

When we were pretty close to the pasture where I was going to leave the bull, Mark Ramsden came up behind Ted. He had been over in the Cold Spring area riding for cattle. He knew something was going on, so he stopped and talked to Ted. When Ted told him the trouble it caused when a rig got close to me, being the nice guy he was and having "been there" himself, Mark didn't want to cause me any trouble so he hung back too until I got right to the gate.

It was after eight o'clock by the time we got the bull into the pasture where we left him. I vowed that I would have a pistol with birdshot before the next fall gather!

Mike was gone to California at the time, so he couldn't come and get the bull right away. With cattle still missing and still drifting down from the higher country, Tom didn't want to shut gates, so I was concerned the bull might go back to where we had found him. He didn't. In a few days Mike got home, so Tom helped him take the bull the rest of the way to Mike's ranch, the B&H, that I wrote about in *My Life on Joseph Creek*.

Down in the steep rugged country on the Imnaha, the bulls brushed up in the bottom of the draws because it got so hot down there. Dwayne packed a pistol with birdshot in it on his belt. He called it "Bull Tamer." When bulls refused to move or got on the fight and started taking our horses, Dwayne shot them in the shoulder or neck to get them to turn and go. The drawback of shooting the bulls was that most of the dogs were very afraid of the gunshots. Most of the time, by the time the bull was moving, the dogs had left us, and we needed them desperately. The cattle knew instantly if you didn't have dogs with you.

Most of the horses didn't like a gun being fired from the rider on his back, either. One of Dwayne's horses, Crook, would scoot off to the side whenever Dwayne raised his arm, after Dwayne had been shooting off him, but he would get over it after a while. The little horse that Dwayne sold to me, Ozzie, didn't jump even when Dwayne shot a 30-30 rifle off him!

Several times I was forced to go off and leave a bull because I simply could not get him to move. When this happened, Dwayne and I would have to go back and get him. With Dwayne shooting him with birdshot we could usually get him to move. After this happening several times, I decided I needed to get a pistol so I could bring in the bulls and Dwayne wouldn't have to go back and get them. After I bought Ozzie and had a horse I could shoot off of, I bought a .22 magnum revolver like the one Dwayne used.

There are more "bull stories" to come, near the end of Part Three in "Fall and Winter 2015-2016," and in "Spring 2016."

PART THREE
RIDING FOR THE 3V RANCH

The Call

When I was teaching in the Enterprise school system I had the privilege of teaching a little country boy, Challis Gorbet, who was a delightful little boy. With my background of having been raised on a ranch in the canyons, he and I talked a lot about riding horses and driving cattle.

He must have gone home and told his dad about some of our conversations because his dad, Wes Gorbet, called me the spring of 2006 and asked if I wanted to help move cattle out in The Divide Country. Of course I jumped at the chance.

We gathered cattle in the Three Buck area. We then drove them around The Cat's Back and ended up in a pasture on The Divide. Little did I know that years later I would be helping Dwayne put cattle in his pasture just across the fence.

It was in March of 2013 when I got a phone call that opened up a whole new area of riding experience for me. Carol Voss, one of the gals that I taught with for years at the Enterprise Elementary School gave me a call.

Carol, and her husband Dwayne own a ranch in the Wallowa Valley, where they live. This place is headquarters for their entire ranching operation. In addition to their own place they lease hundreds more acres in the valley where they raise crops and graze cattle.

They have another place in the open hills, on the edge of the Zumwalt Prairie. The main drainage for this place is a large canyon, Brushy Canyon, which drains into Little Sheep Creek, on the highway to Imnaha. They have range land out on The Divide for summer pasture.

Homer, Wes, and Challis Gorbet

Cattle on the divide. Dwayne owns pasture with the buildings.

Wes and Homer, Gorbet, me, and Norman Pratt

The winter range for the cattle operation is down on lower Imnaha. To the southeast, the rangeland starts about four miles up Horse Creek at a canyon called Cold Camp. The rangeland comes down Horse Creek, taking in the benches on both sides of the canyon. The eastern border for this range is Haas Ridge, and on the west is Grizzly Ridge. Grizzly Ridge ends by dropping down and forming Rye Bench at the place where Horse Creek dumps into the Imnaha. This large bench was once cultivated, as were most of the benches in this area.

Looking up Horse Creek from Cold Camp pasture

Rye Bench is large enough to have an airstrip, which Dwayne made by dragging a spring tooth and a harrow behind a tractor. He set his eyes on the Buckhorn Lookout, miles away across the Imnaha Canyon, perched out on a point above Thorn Creek. By keeping his eyes on the lookout he was able to drive in a straight line, thus making an adequate airstrip for small aircraft.

From the mouth of Horse Creek, the range continues north for several miles on both sides of the Imnaha Canyon. On the east

Looking across at Horse Creek west benches

side it continues north through many benches, which are separated by deep, steep gorges. Dwayne's range ends at a drift fence on the bench at the north end of Haas Ridge. On the other side of this fence is Lightning Creek, which is part of the McClaran rangeland. The cliffs of Haas Ridge form a natural boundary the full length of these east benches, preventing the cattle from topping out.

On the west side of the Imnaha River the range starts right across from the mouth of Horse creek. This pasture is called the "Maggie Beecher Pasture," which to me implies there is a story, but no one knows what it is.

The west side is made up of many benches, canyons and draws which include Corral Creek with all of its tributaries and benches, Thorn Creek with its benches, and the benches between Thorn Creek and Tully Creek. The range extends to the top. Unlike the benches on the east side of the Imnaha, on this west side there are canyons, which the cattle can work their way up until they top out.

Looking across at Rye Bench where the airstrip is located

Looking down Imnaha from School Flat Pasture. Dwayne's range extends to farthest "yellow streak."

Looking across at Haas Ridge and the East Benches, from Maggie Beecher

Maggie Beecher Pasture. Imnaha Canyon on left, Corral Creek on right.

Division fence between McClaran's and Dwayne

Looking across at Corral Creek benches and basin

Looking past hawks on snag, and down on School Flat

Looking across at Thorn Creek. Note bare and green where it had burned.

Tully Creek. Rocky Point in foreground is from where the cover picture for this book was taken.

Looking across at benches between Corral Creek and Thorn Creek

Looking across at Tully Creek. Note fire line, above which burned.

Many of the places the cattle go are so steep, or the ledges so narrow that it is not safe to go horseback. When this happens, the riders go as far as possible on horses, usually trying to get above the cattle, then one rider will get off and hike/slide down the hillside through the rims, with his dogs. He will then grade the cattle around until they eventually come to a canyon bottom where the cattle can go down.

From top of Stubblefield Ridge, looking across Dodson to lower end of Million Dollar Ridge

Meanwhile the other rider will take the horses back the way they came until he comes to the canyon and go down the canyon to where the two riders meet up at the place where the cattle came into the canyon. The cowboy who was afoot is reunited with his horse. Riders and cattle then proceed down the canyon, eventually arriving at the benches. The use of radios makes it much easier to keep track of each other and meet up in the right place.

All of this I learned in the next few years after that initial phone call from Carol. When Carol called me I knew something exciting and adventuresome was about to happen. Her opening remarks were, "Now Julie, I don't want you to feel any pressure. Please feel free to say no if you aren't comfortable with this." She then went on to tell me that one of their cows had died while calving right next to the river. She had gotten on her back and couldn't get up, so both she and the calf died.

The Oregon Department of Fish and Game and the Nez Perce Tribe were both insisting that this dead cow be removed, since she was right by a popular fishing hole. She was across the river from the road and there was no way to get any equipment over there to drag her away from the river.

Dwayne and Carol knew that I had Mattie and Lucie, my team of Belgian molly mules. Dwayne wondered if I would consider using the mules to try to pull the cow away from the river. I told Carol that I would be glad to try, and to have Dwayne give me a call.

Dwayne called me and we started making plans. It was March and I generally didn't start riding for the Birkmaier Ranch until in April so my saddle horse was not shod. I would need a horse to ride across the Imnaha River. Dwayne assured me that he had a horse I could ride, and the horse would do fine fording the river. The agreed-upon day arrived and Dwayne came by with his pickup and trailer to pick me up. I had the mules harnessed and had gathered up the single trees and the double tree that would be needed. Dwayne had the saddle horses we would need. I threw in my saddle. I would saddle the horse I was to ride, Drifter, when we got there.

The dead cow was a few miles down the Imnaha from the mouth of Horse Creek so it took a couple of hours to get there from the valley.

We unloaded the horses and mules and started saddling. We hung the mules' bridles and lines over the hames and tied them on. The single trees and the double tree were tied to the harnesses along the sides of the mules.

I put Mattie in front, to lead her. I ran Lucie's lead rope through the "spider" on Mattie's harness then tied off to Mattie's hames. I gave Lucie a pretty long lead so she wouldn't be right on Mattie's heels. She would be out behind Mattie far enough to be able to see rocks and know where to put her feet.

Here is where I made my first mistake! I don't know what I was thinking—maybe I wasn't. When leading more than one pack animal, I tied each animal to the one in front of it, with a quick release knot to a "break-away" cord. This way if one animal got in trouble I could get it loose from the one it was tied to, and also release any animal tied to the one that is in trouble.

That day when I tied Lucie to Mattie's hames I did it by throwing a couple of half-hitches around the hames.

Having previously decided to sell Mattie and Lucie, I had pictures of them doing all sorts of things, but not fording a river. I took my camera along that day and explained to Dwayne why I would like to get some pictures of them fording the river and also dragging the dead cow.

Dwayne took the camera and told me to watch where he forded the river then to come across just like he had. He put his horse off the bank and into the river, went straight across, staying above a large rock that the water was rushing over. He then turned down stream, went about 150 feet and climbed up the bank on the other side. He was in a good position to take some pictures so I started across.

Maybe I should have been nervous about the whole thing, but I wasn't. Here I was, riding a horse I had never ridden before, fording a river I had never forded, and leading two mules that had never forded a river of this size! I had no reservations as my horse slipped off the bank and into the water. We headed across the river, following the route Dwayne had taken.

This was when I made a second mistake—a near fatal mistake! When leading horses or mules, it is very important you really pay attention to all that is going on around you, to keep an eye on the animals you are leading. It was especially important that day because of Mattie and Lucie having never forded a river before.

I guess I just cast aside all I knew and was only thinking of "looking good" for the pictures Dwayne would be taking. I looked at him rather than turn and see what the mules were doing.

Because they had not forded a river, they couldn't "read the river." They didn't know that the rapids, ripples, and swirls were all telling of the condition of the riverbed, the size of the rocks on the bottom. When there was a really large rock in the river the water would build up against the upriver side then gush over the rock with such force it generally caused a hole to form at the base of the rock on the downriver side.

As we crossed the river we went about eight or ten feet on the upriver side of the large rock. Because I wasn't paying attention to the mules I didn't notice they were drifting downriver from me. Animals will drift downriver as they cross because of the force of the rushing water against them.

Mattie drifted downriver from me, and because I had tied Lucie with a long lead she was able to go down stream even farther than Mattie. Lucie had no idea of what she was doing as she let herself drift down onto the huge rock. She lost her footing and the force of the water washed her over the rock and into the hole below. At one moment all I saw was her nose, with flared nostrils, sticking out of the water. With her floundering, and the buoyancy of the water, Mattie was able to pull her out of the deepest part of the hole.

Just after I pulled Lucie out of the deep hole

When Dwayne realized I was in trouble, he snapped a picture then chucked the camera in a pocket and headed toward me. The Imnaha River gets warm enough in the summer that algae form on the rocks, making them very slick and slimy. Since this was in March, there had been no high water to scour the rocks clean of algae from the previous summer so they were still very slick.

As I tried to lead Mattie forward, thus pulling on Lucie, Lucie tried several times to get her feet under her. Each time she did this, Mattie was able to pull her a little farther from the hole.

Dwayne was riding Crook, who was only four years old at that time. By the time he got to us, Lucie had given up even trying to get up. Dwayne thought he would ride up close to Lucie and pop her with the end of his lariat rope. He hoped this would cause her to try again to get up.

Well, Crook wanted no part of it! Here was a big-headed, long-eared thing, with hames sticking up out of the water. Dwayne couldn't get him within twelve to fifteen feet of Lucie. Crook had pulled many a calf to the branding fire and had stretched cows for doctoring out on the range so he knew how to pull. We decided if we could get Lucie's lead rope untied from Mattie's hames, Dwayne would dally it on his saddle horn and maybe Crook could pull her enough to make her try again to get up.

I had tied her with a couple of half-hitches and Lucie was pulling so hard on the rope, there was no way we could get the lead rope untied. Dwayne said, "We are going to have to cut that rope."

"Go ahead," was my immediate response!

Because I had strung the lead rope up through the spider of Mattie's harness, I thought I would catch it before it could go back through the spider when Dwayne cut it. I rode my horse back along the side of Mattie and reached out to grab the rope, but because this lead rope was all that was holding Lucie's head above the water there was a lot of pressure on it.

When Dwayne cut that rope, it shot back through the spider at such a speed I didn't even have time to close my hand before it was gone. Lucie's head went under water and instantly Dwayne jumped off his horse, grabbed the lead rope and pulled her head out of the water. He tried to pull her head back around over her side, hoping to get her to try to get up.

The Imnaha River heads up in the high Wallowa Mountains. At that time of year, the water was extremely cold. Dwayne and I both knew Lucie had been in the water long enough for hypothermia to be setting in. She had given up completely and was going to just lie there and die!

Dwayne had stock dogs that were jaw-dropping impressive. He had five or six of them with him that day. They had swum across the river and were intently watching from the bank.

I looked at the dogs then at Dwayne. "Will your dogs come out in the water?" He said they would.

So I said, "Sic 'em on her."

Dwayne called his dogs in and they literally attacked Lucie. They were grabbing and biting everything that was sticking up out of the water. One dog actually stuck his mouth under the water to grab her.

Getting the team ready

This probably didn't last more than a few moments, but it seemed like an eternity! I had just thought, "This isn't going to work," when Lucie seemed to explode and scrambled to her feet. Dwayne led her to shore and tied her to a river willow.

After letting her stand a little while Dwayne tried to lead her along the edge of the river to where he could go up the bank and out of the river. Lucie refused to re-enter the water so Dwayne had to break his way through the river willows along the bank.

Pulling the dead cow

When we were regrouped and the mules were tied to a hackberry tree, I started getting the harness ready to pull the cow. I had to bridle the mules, string the lines, and hook up the double and single trees. We felt fortunate that we had not lost any of these throughout the whole ordeal.

Lucie was cold and trembling like a leaf. She stood and shivered the whole time I was getting them ready. I was glad I had some work for her to do, to help her warm up. Many animals will not go anywhere near a carcass, especially if it is starting to get "ripe." As was so typical of my mules, they backed up to the dead cow as easily as if we were going to drag a log to a campfire.

The cow needed pulled from the flat place next to the river, up a bank, then along a little bench. Lucie was doing her best, but simply wasn't able to give it 100% after all that had happened. They pulled the cow along the flat by the river, but when they started up the bank, though both of the mules were giving it all they could, they simply couldn't get the cow all the way up the bank. Dwayne came with Crook, put his rope on the cow and dallied up, then with all three of them pulling they were able to get her up the bank onto the bench.

When the job was finished I unbridled the mules, took off the lines, and tied the double and single trees back on the harnesses of the mules. I switched the lead ropes on the mules so the short one that we had cut was on Mattie. I tied Lucie onto Mattie again and headed for the river wondering how Lucie would react to entering the water.

Coming back across the Imnaha—a different route!

Where we entered the river, there was a large flat rock so Lucie was unable to set her feet as she could have in dirt or a sandy beach. She wasn't real excited to enter the river, but Mattie pulled her in and once in the water she was fine.

Since the photo session had not gone too well on the way over we decided to try it again. Dwayne went ahead of me so he could get pictures of the mules crossing the river. This time we took a route that took us below the rock.

As we drove home that night we relived the whole episode. We both thought for sure that we were going to lose Lucie. I had stayed amazingly calm throughout the whole ordeal, and though it was never verbalized, I wondered if Dwayne wasn't at least a little surprised or impressed that I did not panic—that I had kept my head and stayed cool.

Regardless of Dwayne's summation of the whole encounter, that was the beginning of my riding for him in that wonderfully beautiful, steep, rugged country. Little did I know what exciting, breathtaking experiences were to occur in the next few years!

Spring 2013

I have always loved riding in new country. *Driving* through a new area is like viewing an uncut pie. It's beautiful and inviting, but *riding* an area is like cutting that pie and getting into the filling. It would be an understatement to say I was excited when Dwayne called me and asked if I would be interested in riding for him! Because Dwayne's cattle are "on grass" year 'round and his cattle graze in such a widespread area, it is necessary to ride 250 days a year, or more.

Not long after the mule incident, Dwayne called and asked me to help move cattle around on the benches east of Horse Creek. Some of the cattle were in the East Pasture, a pasture that extends from the north end of Haas Ridge back upcountry toward Horse Creek.

Cows and elk in rims of East Pasture

The Snake River pack of wolves were coming down Lightning Creek, around the point at the north end of Haas Ridge, then back around the benches of the East Pasture. Dwayne wanted to gather the breaks and benches of this pasture and push the cattle south toward Horse Creek to hopefully keep them away from the wolves.

Mountain sheep in East Pasture

A few cattle were still scattered in the rims on the west side of the river or were hanging along the canyon bottom on the east side. These cattle needed pushed up to the benches on the east side where they would stay until most of the calving was done. Most of the cattle were in the School Flat Pasture, which was on the east side of the Imnaha from the mouth of Horse Creek on down the Imnaha canyon for several miles, in the Middle Pasture, which was on the east benches of Horse Creek from the mouth of Horse Creek and up Horse Creek a couple of miles, and in the

East Pasture breaks with animal trails terracing hillside, which is called "honeycombing."

Dwayne on Drifter, riding river-rim trail

Coming down point in Maggie Beecher to Horse Creek Bridge

Cold Camp Pasture, which ran on up Horse Creek a couple of miles past the upper end of the Middle Pasture. A few cattle were also on the west benches up Horse Creek. We rode for several days and got the cattle pretty well situated. In fact, we did so well, we got the job finished a day earlier than expected.

I had taken my pickup and horse trailer down with my horse and dogs. Dwayne said that I might as well go home—he could handle what was left to do.

Dwayne, pushing cattle up the Bull Trail

Grading around through the rims

On the bull trail

Up in rims of Cold Camp Pasture. Note cattle below.

Dwayne bringing cattle up in the East Pasture

Cattle on School Flat

Walking Cane and Grizzly Ridges across Horse Creek, as seen from the Middle Pasture

Bringing cattle out of Horse Creek West Benches

Cow Camp, as seen from breaks of Horse Creek West Benches

As seen from up on the breaks of Grizzly Ridge, Rye Bench, with airstrip in foreground; School Flat across canyon; in far distance, the benches of Thorn and Tully Creeks

Gathering cattle from the breaks of the Rye Bench Pasture. Note intersection of the Imnaha and Horse Creek roads.

Gathering cattle from hillside where bulls slid to their death

The day after I left, Dwayne was involved in a serious accident. He was hospitalized for several weeks. He was finally sent home with instructions to do no riding for several weeks, then to ride only at a walk—no running the horse or riding in rough terrain. He was still packing some hardware! Of course he did more than he should have, even though I did a lot of riding for him as he healed up.

After most of the cattle had calved it was time to gather and push the cattle back across the Horse Creek Bridge and up onto the west benches. There was a lot of area to ride. These east bench pastures contained a lot of gullies and draws which made it easy to miss cattle if it wasn't ridden thoroughly.

The cattle were trailed down Horse Creek and pushed up onto the west benches: the Maggie Beecher Pasture, the Corral Creek Benches, and the Thorn Creek Benches. They were left there until it was time to start pushing them up Corral Creek into the Corral Creek Basin.

That spring, 2013, we were gathering the west benches and pushing the cattle above the drift fence in Corral Creek. We were gathering the Maggie Beecher pasture with me

Cattle trailing down Horse Creek, headed for Horse Creek Bridge. Again, note intersection of Imnaha and Horse Creek roads

Pushing cattle up the point to Maggie Beecher

riding the benches and Dwayne riding the breaks.

As I pushed cattle along, there was one cow that seemed to not have a calf. As I was approaching the gate between the Maggie Beecher Pasture and the Corral Creek Benches Pasture, I decided I would drop this cow and let her go back and find her calf.

At about the time I decided to let her go back she took off and went to the front of the bunch. She never came to the back of the bunch again so I thought maybe she had found her calf after all. I met up with Dwayne and we pushed the cattle up Corral Creek and through the drift fence, shutting the gate behind them.

Cow elk in Maggie Beecher

The next day we rode the benches and breaks back toward Thorn Creek and Tully Creek. Again we pushed the cattle up through the drift fence in Corral Creek.

The third day we re-rode the pastures we had ridden the first two days. Dwayne went to the Thorn Creek and Corral Creek Benches and breaks. I re-rode the benches and breaks of the Maggie Beecher Pasture. As I was riding along the benches I heard the faint bawl of a calf up a gully, coming down out of the rims. I gave a "whoop" and the calf bawled again. I started up the bank on the edge of the gully, whooping every so often with the calf seeming to answer me.

There had to be a den nearby.

After going up the hill a ways, I realized, by listening to the bawls of the calf, that it was climbing higher up the gully instead of coming down toward me. My whooping was pushing him higher and higher, so I quit whooping and continued in silence.

I rode Chip until it got so steep he simply could not go any farther. I got off, tied him to a hackberry tree and started climbing the hillside.

It was an overcast day and drizzling a mist—not a real rain, but enough to get you wet without a raincoat—thus I was wearing a slicker. I always wear gloves when I am riding, to protect my hands, as I break limbs when going through the brush.

I could still hear the calf bawling occasionally, and he was still going higher. Natural instinct tells an animal that it gains an advantage against a predator by gaining elevation.

Dwayne on Thunder in the sumac up Corral Creek

Corral Creek buildings from breaks of Corral Creek Pasture. Horse Creek at top of photo

It became so steep that I was grabbing onto bushes to help pull myself up the hillside. After some time, I became so warm I took my slicker off and stopped for a breather. The brim of my hat had kept me from seeing anything above eye level. When I stopped to breathe, I tipped my hat back and looked up the hill. It was then that I discovered that I had been grabbing onto sumac brush, but also poison ivy. Fortunately, I was wearing gloves and long sleeved shirts so I didn't break out with a rash.

I knew the calf could only go so far before the rims would stop his ascent. Sure enough, he finally could climb no farther. He must have felt he was being trapped so he climbed out on a ledge of a rim. I worked my way out on the ledge and threw him back around and off the ledge.

Instead of heading down the gully he then went around under another rim. I followed him around, and again turned him back toward the bottom of the gully. He did then start down the gully, which was full of brush. It was very steep so I had to go very slowly.

After a short while I lost sight of the calf and could not hear him going through the brush. I sent my dogs into the brush, but they came back out onto the open hillside with their noses to the ground. I was just thinking, "What in the world are they doing?" when they found the calf under a bush. The calf then started on down the gully.

I made my way on down to my horse, untied him, and started leading him down the hill. While doing this I saw a lone, black, mature animal coming around the road, down on the benches. It was coming from the direction of Corral Creek so I hopefully thought that most likely it was the calf's mother. By the time I got down the gully and out on the open hillside to where I could see the road where I had last seen the "cow," the cow and calf were both gone. I went on down to the road and tried to read the tracks. It seemed the cow had proceeded on around the road, the wrong way, with the calf beside her.

I started around the road after them. It had continued to rain, so the farther I went the less clear the tracks were and I saw no sign of the critters. I started doubting myself. Maybe those weren't fresh track I had seen. Maybe when the cow and calf reunited they had started back around the right way before I got down to where I could see them.

Calf on ledge of rim

Just as I was about ready to turn around and go back, I heard the calf bawl in the distance. The bawl came from on around the road, in the wrong direction. This was a mixed blessing. Now I knew where they were, but if the calf was with its mother, why was it still bawling?

I hurried along, trying to catch up with them. When I finally got close enough to see what they were, I was surprised to see the "cow" really was a yearling bull. The calf was so glad to see another critter it had "mothered up" to the bull.

I could not get ahead of them by following them on the road. This road went out around a point then back into a draw, again out around a point and again back into a draw. My only chance of getting ahead of them would be to wait until they started out around a point, then I would go up over the ridge, getting ahead of them on the road before they got into the next draw.

I did get ahead of them and started them back toward Corral Creek. The calf went really well until we got to the gully where it had come off the hill. This was apparently where he had last seen his mother and he didn't want to leave this area.

I kept working with them and got them to Corral Creek. As I approached the gate, I noticed there were several pairs and several lone cows on the other side of the fence.

As I put the bull and calf through the gate the calf stuck close to the side of the bull, as though the bull had become his security. The calf did not even look at the cows. The bull and calf walked about three feet in front of one of the cows. As they passed the cow, she gave a "moo" and the calf swung around and almost in the same motion grabbed a teat and started sucking. This cow was a young cow that hadn't had the courage to breech the fence and go back looking for her baby. An old cow would have crawled through the fence and gone back to the last place she had seen her calf.

If the calf had not been found and had been left on the benches he would have become coyote food because we weren't going to ride that area again. Oh, the satisfaction of things turning out right!

After the cattle were pushed above the Corral Creek drift fence they were left to work their way to the top. They also graded out on the hillsides and ridges. They were left in this pasture until the time came to gather them and start the long move to Brushy.

Some of the old-time cowboys would say that if you try to move a herd of more than two hundred pairs, you have just made your first mistake of the drive. There were between 450 and 500 cows in the Corral Creek Pasture, with the majority having already calved. Dwayne tried to divide the herd in half for the drive to the Chesnimnus Cow Camp Pasture by first gathering just the cattle that were hanging along the top.

It was May 22nd and time to start moving the cattle toward the Vance Drawn pasture. We trailered out to the head of Corral creek. It had snowed two or three inches of wet, heavy snow the night before so it kept balling up on our horses' feet. We were glad we weren't going down into the steep country because even on top the horses had trouble keeping their feet under them. It continued to snow on us most of the day.

Gathering cattle at top of Corral Creek Basin

When Dwayne decided we had gathered enough cattle, the gate was opened and we headed for the Chesnimnus Pasture. We drove the cattle there by going down the Zumwalt Road past Thomason Meadows a couple of miles, then went west over a hill to the pasture.

At Thomason Meadows, headed for Vance Draw

We dropped into the head of Chesnimnus Creek just above the old Chesnimnus Cow Camp. After the cattle were put in the pasture we had to stay with them to make sure they were all mothered up—when the cows find their calves. When the cattle were put in each of these pastures, which had an abundance of fresh grass, the cows were so intent on their grazing, they totally disregarded the whereabouts of their calves. They generally didn't start looking for their calves until they were full, which could take hours.

Cattle in pasture near old Chesnimnus Cow Camp

Meanwhile the calves were sure that their mothers were still back in the pasture we just came from, so they were determined to head back to that pasture. We had to stay with the herd for as much as four hours, waiting for all the pairs to get mothered up. The cows with very young calves were usually better about keeping track of their babies.

We then loaded up and trailered back to the valley. When we were almost to Dwayne's place in the valley he looked at the clock in the dash of the pickup and said, "Gosh Julie, we have been at it only sixteen hours today, but don't worry I'll pay you for a full day anyway!"

The next morning, we trailered back out to the head of the Corral Creek Basin and gathered the breaks and down in the canyons. It wasn't snowing and yesterday's snow had melted.

The Corral Creek Basin was comprised of Corral Creek with its forks and two other sizeable canyons—Stubblefield and Dodson. Dwayne and I rode the hillsides and ridges. We pushed the cattle into the bottoms of the canyons and onto the ridge tops where other riders picked them up and pushed them to the top.

Stubblefield "heads" some distance under the summit of the basin. To get to it from the top, we went down a neighboring ridge then side-hilled around to the head of Stubblefield. The head of Stubblefield was so steep we got off and led our horses for a ways. After we had gone about a quarter of a mile, it became a little less steep so we were able to remount and ride. Though it is not the largest canyon in the basin, it has some interesting history.

Dwayne by old Chesnimnus Cow Camp

Looking down into Stubblefield

After going into Stubblefield for the first time, I started telling Jean Stubblefield Cook about it. Jean had lived on the Imnaha for years when she and her deceased husband, Jim, ranched down there. The Stubblefield canyon was named after one of Jim's ancestors, "Uncle Billy" Stubblefield. Jean asked me if I had seen "Uncle Billy's" dugout. Of course I didn't even know what she was talking about so she told me the following story.

Uncle Billy Stubblefield had homesteaded up Horse Creek. It is said that he planted 80 to 100 different kinds of fruit trees throughout the region. He was a very colorful character. It is also said that he had four wives and twenty-some children!

It seems that Uncle Billy had herded sheep up in "Stubblefield" in the late 1800s. There were a few grizzly bears in that area at that time, thus the name, Grizzly Ridge, on the east side of the Imnaha River. Because of this, Uncle Billy dug a hole in the hillside, somewhere up Stubblefield, big enough to sleep in with his rifle. He piled limbs and branches over the entry to the hole each night after he crawled in. He figured that he would hear a bear breaking in and would have time to shoot the bear before it could kill him.

Each time Dwayne and I went up or down through Stubblefield we tried to find anything that looked like it could have been Uncle Billy's "hole." Figuring Uncle Billy would have slept close to where he bedded his sheep for the night narrowed the possibilities of where the hole could have been. There weren't many places in the canyon where he could have bedded sheep. Even at that, we were not able to locate the "dugout."

You can read more about Uncle Billy Stubblefield in *The History of Wallowa County, Oregon*, copyright 1983, pp. 93-94.

There is another piece of interesting history, which occurred in the Corral Creek Basin. Up Corral Creek a mile or so above the mouth of the Stubblefield canyon there is a waterfall, which made it impossible to have a trail up the bottom of the canyon. About three-quarters of a mile below the falls, the Indians made a trail up a ridge, then graded around the rims, above some high cliffs, through a niche in a high rim, and back into the bottom of Corral Creek just above the falls.

Legend has it that in the 1800s one band of Indians waited in the niche and ambushed another band, massacring all of them, then threw their bodies over the cliff. There were battles between the Wallowa Valley Indians and the Snake Indians on a regular basis. Joe McClaran says that when he first went into that part of the country, in the 1920s, bones could still been seen down on the rockslide below the cliff. It now is so overgrown with brush that the rockslide can hardly be seen.

Niche in rims at head of Indian Trail

This "Indian Trail" is narrow and a little scary in places. Since the time of the Indians, someone blasted a trail through the cliff and around the falls so cattle could be driven up the bottom of the canyon. Dwayne stashed de-icer in a cave nearby to put on the trail when it iced up, so cattle wouldn't slip off the trail.

Looking back at niche, showing rims and brush the trail goes through!

Looking down at Corral Creek Benches from Niche

He told me about the trail and asked if I would like to go on it. Of course I would!

The Corral Creek Basin was entirely steep, rugged country. To get to cattle that were not more than a half mile away "as the crow flies," at times we had to ride two to three miles. The use of radios saved a lot of time and effort. Many times we could not see a cow on the ridge we were riding because she was above or below a rim, thus being hidden from our view. One of us, on the next ridge over, could see the cow and radio the other rider and tell him of the cow. At times like this, the radios were "worth their weight in gold."

When the cattle were gathered and pushed to the top of the Corral Creek Basin some of the riders would stay with them and "hold them," keeping them from scattering, while other riders did more riding, if it had been determined that some back riding was needed. When we had gathered all of the cattle we could find, we again headed for the Chesnimnus Pasture where we had put cattle the day before. Then of course, we had to spend several hours getting them mothered up before we headed home. Again when we were almost to Dwayne's, he looked at the clock as he had the night before and said, "My gosh Julie, we have only put in fourteen hours today! There must be *some* fence we can work on for a while!" Oh, that sense of humor!

The cattle were left in that pasture for a few days then we pushed them over one more ridge to the Vance Draw pasture. They stayed there until Dwayne decided it was time to start the long drive to Brushy.

Looking into north fork of Stubblefield. Note cattle on bench.

Cattle in Vance Draw Pasture

Sharon, Dwayne, and Cannon Ball, doctoring a foot-rot cow

Sherry and Sharon eating lunch

When it was time to start the three-day drive from Vance Draw to Brushy we gathered the Vance Draw Pasture then moved the cattle to the Elephant Corrals. Even though it was a short drive mile-wise, it could prove to be very frustrating. After the cattle were gathered and put through the gate

105

leaving the pasture, they were driven up a draw that was full of timber and brush. The draw had a little dirt road just out of the bottom.

We were pushing cattle up this draw and about thirty or forty calves were at the rear of the herd, trying to go back to the pasture. I was up on the hill above the road pushing some cows and calves while Dwayne was pushing some on the road. One little calf, who was only a couple of days old, suddenly turned back and started down the road. If Dwayne left the big group of calves to go after the one he could lose thirty or forty calves, so he just kept going with the bunch. I was busy and didn't even see the little guy go back. Then a couple of older calves turned back. Dwayne sent the dogs after them, but the dogs couldn't get them. Very seldom does a calf get away from Dwayne's dogs.

We kept pushing the cattle and put them in the Elephant Corral Pasture then started the mothering-up process. After several hours Dwayne had to make the decision of which cows really

Elephant Corral Pasture

needed to go back for the calves that had gone back, and which cows were just messing around—not looking for their calves in the herd. He knew the mother to the tiny calf because they had hung to the back most of the time, though she had gone up into the herd just before the calf turned back. Dwayne let her go back, plus a couple more cows. The cows bawled all the way down the draw to the Vance Pasture.

Older calves will walk around bawling, but a tiny baby generally will just lay and wait for the mama to come to him. This works good when the mama has bedded the baby down and knows where he is, but in this case the baby had slipped off and the mama had no idea where he was.

While following the cows back to the pasture, we had looked all along the road for the baby, figuring he probably wouldn't have gone far. We couldn't find him. We followed the cows to the pasture, put the bigger calves that were standing there bawling, with the cows and then started back up the road.

I figured Dwayne didn't need my help following them up the road so I pulled up about 150 feet above the road and started going through the timber and brush. I tried to stay where I could see all of the area between me, and the road that Dwayne was on.

As little as the calf was, I figured he surely wouldn't go up the hill farther than where I was. While going along I prayed, "God if that little guy is here, please let me see him."

I had gone a little farther when I saw the silhouette of little ears and the top of a little head. The calf was lying in a dark place under the thick boughs of a spruce tree. With the calf being black, all I could see was the outline of his head against the light grass in the background.

I yelled, "Dwayne, there is a calf up here!" Dwayne left the cows he was following and came up to where I was.

If calves are afraid, they will mother-up to your horse, sometimes getting right under the horse's belly. Dwayne knew if he could get the calf to mother-up to his horse, it would follow him to the corral. Dwayne put his dogs on the calf. I don't think they even bit it, but the calf was so scared it let out one big 'beller' and headed for Dwayne's horse. Dwayne started down the hill toward the road, with the calf following, but he had not gone more than fifteen or twenty feet when up through the brush, the mama came for her baby. She had heard the one beller the calf had given and she came to rescue him. Another baby had been saved from being coyote food!

Headed for Brushy via the Zumwalt Road

The Zumwalt school in its last days

At Midway

The trip from the Elephant Corrals to Brushy was pretty uneventful with just the usual challenges of keeping the cattle that are in pastures along the road from jumping in with ours. It really was quite spectacular seeing the cattle strung out for miles as we crossed the Zumwalt Prairie! We saw deer and herds of elk all along the way.

Heading for Brushy, going cross-country

Crossing Box Canyon

We left the Zumwalt Road at Midway and went cross-country for about four miles before reaching Dwayne's Brushy Pasture where the cattle would be left until they were gathered for branding.

We had gathered Brushy and were sorting cattle for branding in the flats on Little Sheep Creek, at the mouth of Brushy. The flats were divided into three lots, or small pastures. We were sorting off pairs in one direction and cows that hadn't calved in another.

We worked the cattle very slowly, keeping them calm. In fact, they were so settled, many of them were lying down. We would ease in and find a pair then quietly work them out of the herd and put them through the gate, or we would find a dry cow—a cow who had not yet had her calf—and work her out of the herd.

We had been sorting for quite some time when a dry cow started giving us trouble. We could get her out of the group and started for the gate, but then she would whirl around and run back into the group. We let her get away with it a couple of times because there were plenty of others that needed sorted, and we didn't want to charge into the herd and stir up the whole bunch.

After a time, Dwayne cut the same old cantankerous cow out again and started for the gate. As usual she went just fine for a little ways, then she did the old "turn-back trick." Dwayne had had enough of her, so he spurred Crook into a gallop, trying to head her off before she got back into the group. He was still not supposed to be doing any hard riding!

She ran into the group with Dwayne in hot pursuit. There was a cow standing broadside, right where Dwayne needed to go to head off the cow, so he thought he would just go around the rear end of her. Just as he did this, another cow, which had not been in view because she was lying down, started to get up. There was no time to stop or change direction, so Crook "T-boned" her. This caused Crook to tumble.

All I could see was Dwayne being catapulted through mid-air and all four of Crook's legs sticking up in the air. I thought, "Oh, my gosh, he is going to roll right over Dwayne!" I went galloping up to where they were. By the time I got to them, Dwayne and Crook were both on their feet. The McCarty rope was still tucked in Dwayne's belt and Crook was circling around him. Crook had never been "in a wreck" before so it had scared him as much as it did me!

Dwayne was standing stooped over with his hands on his knees. As I rode up to him he drawled, "I still have hardware in me from the last wreck. I'm not supposed to be having any more wrecks. That must have been quite a sight! Where's a camera when you need it?" After standing for a little while, Dwayne remounted and we continued to sort cattle! He's a tough ol' bird!

After branding, the cattle would be taken to The Divide for the summer. By the time the cattle had arrived at The Divide they would have traveled 65 miles from the benches in the East Pasture and up Horse Creek.

Dwayne didn't need me to help with the branding and he and his crew were able to do all of the riding from this time on through the summer. He wouldn't need me again until fall or winter, much to my chagrin!

The Freeze of 2013-2014

There are stories of the terrible winter of 1919. The Snake River froze over and they got twelve-to-eighteen inches of snow even in the bottoms of the Snake River and Salmon River canyons. The cattle were out on winter range, and the ranchers had no hay to feed them—couldn't have gotten it to the cattle even if they did have it. Cattle died by the thousands. Ranchers went broke.

Considering what we know about that winter I guess the winter of 2013-2014 wasn't quite as bad as it seemed to some of us who are a couple of generations too young to have experienced 1919. Nevertheless, it was the worst winter in the canyons for maybe thirty years. It was quite common for the canyon to freeze up once, but not several times, one right after the other. In that steep country the cattle simply couldn't get around if the ground froze hard. They couldn't get footing, so slid until something stopped them.

In the open country, like Dwayne's winter range, there was nothing to stop them except an occasional bush, or the bottom of a draw, gully, or swale. If none of these were present, they slid to their death. Once they start sliding, they usually would face downhill and "plant" their feet, trying to stop themselves. I have had more than one person say that when they start sliding, they beller and bawl as if they were in a squeeze chute. They know what's coming!

Not all slides were fatal. After the freezes of the winter of 2013-2014, the hills on Dwayne's winter range were covered with slide marks. It looked as if a Paul Bunyan-sized trowel had raked almost every slope. No matter where we were, we could look around and see skid marks somewhere.

Example of slide marks (I lost my camera with the good photos!)

The thing that allowed Dwayne to have a minimum number of fatal slides was that in so much of the area there was a gully or draw at the base of the steep slopes. The slopes that were rocky with rims weren't where the best grass was, so the cattle usually were in the places with better grass, so when they slid they ended up in a draw, which usually wasn't fatal. When we saw new slide marks we looked in the bottom to see if a dead animal was there. When the conditions were like this, the ranchers left the cattle alone—they didn't even try to move them because of possibly causing a cow to slide.

As soon as the conditions improved somewhat, Dwayne and I started gathering and moving cattle. Our horses were sharp shod, but even at that, they would slip and slide even when we were riding across the benches. When the ground wasn't frozen, we generally avoided riding the rocky south hillsides because it was so hard for the horses to travel through all the rocks. We rode ridge tops and the north slopes of the draws where there was better soil, thus easier for the horses to walk.

During "the freeze" the safest places to ride were the souths, because they weren't frozen so hard and the horse's feet didn't slip as much when going over rocky ground—unless they stepped on a big, smooth, sloping rock.

I had gathered the benches of the Maggie Beecher Pasture and had started back with a bunch of cattle. At one place I could see down into the head of a draw. There were a few cattle bedded on a little flat so I started hollering at them. They started moving. They could see the cattle I was driving, so wanted to join them, but as is the case in most draws, it was very steep at the top of the draw. I sat and waited for them to pick their way up the slope. It took some time, but they made it. That is, all but one. As she started up the slope she lost her footing and slid back into the bottom of the draw. Fortunately, there was a flat, smooth place where she came to rest. She stood up then became a "statue." She wasn't about to try it again!

After I had gotten my bunch where they belonged, I rode back around the benches to pick up anything I might have missed, or that Dwayne had pushed up out of the draws.

It so happened that I was at the head of the draw where the cow had slid when I saw Dwayne coming up it with some cows he had found down lower. I waited at the top for him. When his cows got to the "statue" they went right by her and started picking their way out of the draw.

When Dwayne came to the "statue" and she didn't move, he told his dogs to push her up. We had radios so I told him what had happened previously. He knew she wouldn't move so he left her. After a critter had slid—if it didn't kill it—it would stand until the ground thawed and it felt it was safe to move. I don't know how long that old cow stayed in that draw, but it was weeks before she came trailing in to the mouth of Horse Creek.

Another day I was riding in the Maggie Beecher Pasture. I looked over to Rye Bench where Dwayne's bulls were wintering. They did fine as long as they stayed on the bench or the slope above it, but if they got on the steep hillside that sloped down into Horse Creek, they more than likely would slide.

There was a bull just under the top of this steep hillside. I thought, "What are you doing, you crazy ol' guy? You had better get off of there before you slide." I went on riding then sometime later I thought of the bull and looked back over toward Rye Bench. The bull was gone. I hoped he had made it off okay.

We had trailered to the mouth of Horse Creek that day. When the day's work was finished, we loaded up and started up Horse Creek to cow camp. I remembered the bull being in that dangerous place so when we got to where I could see that slope, I was looking closely. Sure enough, I could see skid marks. I asked Dwayne to stop, pointed out the skid marks, and told him of seeing the bull earlier that day.

Dwayne said sure enough, those were new skid marks. He walked over to where he could see the other side of Horse Creek through the brush and trees. There at the bottom of the slope lay the bull, dead.

Hillside where two bulls slid to their death

From the skid marks we could see that the bull had slid until he hit a rim. This rim's edge had an outcropping that stuck up about three or four feet above the edge of the rim. The bull had hit this rock head on, which probably killed him instantly. The momentum of his body caused it to swing around the side of this rock and tumble over the cliff. He then continued to roll and slide on down, and topple over yet another rim. His body then went on to the bottom where the trees and brush stopped it. A few weeks earlier another bull had done about the same thing, just at a different location. The loss of two bulls is not

The hillside on the Horse Creek side of Rye Bench

a good thing, but thankfully that is all Dwayne lost. A neighbor on down the Imnaha lost between twenty-five and thirty cows. A rancher down Joseph Creek at one point had eight cows slide to their death and end up in the road—no telling how many more he lost in the canyons before it thawed.

Dwayne's son and daughter helped us move cattle whenever they could get free. Will worked for the ranch full time so had many other responsibilities. Erin lived and worked in La Grande, but came up and helped quite often. Dwayne had the ranch's hired man, Will Cannon—alias Cannon Ball—also help move cattle whenever we needed more riders.

Spring came and we did the usual gathering and moving of cattle. After the cattle were driven from Corral

Will on Duke, Dwayne on Crook, Erin on Drifter

Creek to Brushy and the brandings were completed, they were put on the east side of Little Sheep Creek. After a few weeks it was time to move them to The Divide for the summer. Dwayne had pushed the cattle to the top, so we had to just gather the top. It was going to be a hot day so we got a very early start. We wanted to make the climb to the top before the sun rose so the dogs and horses wouldn't get so hot.

All went as planned, and it was a beautiful day. It was my first time helping on this leg of the journey to summer pasture. I was thrilled to see new country and of course I took many photos.

Cannon Ball on Duke, with Dot

Note dogs near cattle in mid upper photo. They are working a half-mile away!

My three helpers: Chip, Jo and Paige

Paige looking for cattle

Sheepherder Monument in Brushy

Doctoring calf at Elephant Corral Pasture

Wallowa Mountains from top of Devil's Ridge

Headed for The Divide

Jo, waiting for a command

FALL AND WINTER 2014-2015

On the 3V ranch, Dwayne brought his cattle down from summer pasture on The Divide, weaned the calves then put the cows up Brushy.

On November 18th we started gathering Brushy so we could start the long trek north that would end at Buckhorn and down into the breaks of the Corral Creek Basin. The first day we trailered down Little Sheep Creek to the mouth of Brushy. The twins, Sharon Gibson and Sherry Vanlueven were also riding for Dwayne. They don't like the steep places so they stayed in the bottom while Dwayne and I rode the hillsides.

Gathering cattle in Brushy

There was snow in some places so it would ball up on the horses' feet until the "sharp-shoes" could do no good, thus the horses did some slipping on the hillsides. Riding the canyon bottom wasn't all fun either because the sun wasn't hitting down there, so it was really cold for Sharon and Sherry. It is crazy, but some of our coldest temperatures all winter were that third week in November. One morning when I went to the barn to saddle my horse it was two above zero. The next morning it was three above. The highs that week never got above freezing.

Dwayne and Cannon Ball chopping ice at Elephant Corrals

The drive from Brushy to the Elephant Corrals was uneventful. It was cold but clear, so we were thankful there wasn't a blizzard blowing snow in our faces. The day we drove the cattle from the Elephant Corrals to the breaks of Corral Creek, it did snow a little, but there was no wind so it was calm and beautiful.

Leaving Elephant Corrals

A few of the cows had calved early so we had a few babies with us, but they made it fine. When we got to the Corral Creek Basin, we put the cattle through the gate and started pushing them north, around the rim of the basin. We pushed thirty, seventy, or one hundred cows down various ridges, depending on the size of the ridge. We had already pushed several bunches down ridges when Dwayne and I started down yet another ridge with about thirty cows. Sharon and Sherry were going to keep pushing the rest of the cattle on around the rim of the basin.

Because of the steepness, the cattle Dwayne and I were pushing didn't want to go down. We did finally get them down the ridge a ways when we came to a rim right on the crest of the ridge. It seemed the best thing to do was to push them back around the hillside a ways then turn them back under the rim.

The Stein Place

Dwayne was on the ridge, pushing the cattle back around the hillside toward me. I realized it was really getting steep where I was—that I was asking too much of Chip, so I stepped off. When I stepped off, I realized it was even steeper than I had thought. It was so cold that day that I had on a pair of gloves under a pair of mittens. Just before I stepped off, I took my gloves and mittens off, and stuffed them in a horn bag, so I could better use my fingers to loose Chips lead rope. My plan was to undo the lead rope so I could lead Chip. I was using roping reins—reins that attach to the bit on one side then go up over the horse's neck and attach to the bit on the other side.

Thomason Meadows

As I stepped off, I laid the reins on Chip's neck right in front of the saddle. I was going to tie them to the horn just as soon as I got the lead rope off the saddle horn.

This is when the "wreck" commenced. As quick as a flash, Chip put his head down to get a bite of grass then took a step forward, and put his foot through the reins. When he tried to raise his head it yanked on his bit so he whirled and reared. He reared so high it seemed he would go over backwards, but just before he went over backwards, he swung his front end around and down the hill. His front feet hit the ground with such a force it is a

Dwayne on Crook, on Breaks of Corral Creek Basin

miracle he didn't break a leg! This happened with such a momentum it caused his rear end to swing around, again becoming downhill from his front end. This again yanked on his bit and the whole thing started all over again. After several revolutions he stopped, kind of sidewise with the hill. I started down toward him, talking softly and calmly. I got within about fifteen feet of him when he tried to turn his head to look at me. This caused the bit to jerk on his mouth; he reared and once again started down the hill.

I could do nothing but stand and watch. After several more revolutions he stopped with his front feet downhill. I had been wearing a slicker, so ripped it off, knowing I was going to have to hike back up out of there. I started down toward him again, speaking quietly and soothingly. Just as I got to him, out of my peripheral vision I saw Dwayne's arm reach past me, with an open knife. Dwayne slipped the blade in to where the rein was attached to the bit by the use of a piece of leather shoestring. He slit the shoestring and immediately the rein was free from the bit, thus taking the pressure off of Chip's mouth.

Near Joe Clemons cabin, headed for Million Dollar Ridge, near Buckhorn

Pushing cattle down Million Dollar Ridge

Thank goodness Dwayne always carried a very sharp knife in a place he could get to it quickly. Even though Dwayne had been quite a bit farther up the hill than I was, he reached Chip at about the same time as I did. Dwayne amazed me how swiftly and agilely he got around on those steep, rocky slopes!

We got the cattle on down the ridge, leading our horses, then we stopped and Dwayne fixed my reins. Ever since I got into trouble with a broken rein in Cougar Creek years before, which Dave Yost fixed with a piece of shoestring he carried on his saddle, I carried a leather shoestring on my saddle for just such emergencies.

Will, on Drifter

We mounted and our horses carried us to the top where we reunited with Sharon and Sherry. We moved the cattle on around the crest of the basin, putting several more bunches down ridges. As we moved on around toward Buckhorn, the top got so brushy and steep the cattle could not go, so we put them out through a gate into the adjoining pasture. After going about a mile we put the cattle through another gate and back into Dwayne's pasture, then pushed them down Million Dollar Ridge, which is almost directly under Buckhorn. The boys—Will and Canon Ball—had brought their horses and rigs around so they helped us with the last part of the drive. Dwayne built a fire and we stood around it for a while to warm up and discuss the day's events. Dwayne and the boys made plans for the next day then we loaded up and started the long drive back to the valley.

The next day Dwayne and I trailered to the Vance Draw Pasture. We gathered twenty-five bulls and started for Thomason Meadows. When we got to Thomason Meadows we headed cross-country for several miles, going in an easterly direction. Our destination was the breaks in the head of Log Creek.

Dwayne and Will had taken the bulls on this same route the year before and it proved to be quite a job because the bulls had no idea where they were going. When we headed cross-country from Thomason Meadows, Dwayne said, "I wonder if these ol' boys will know the way!" The route changed direction several times due to topography and fences. Each time we came to a place where we had to change direction, Dwayne wondered if the bulls would make the turn. We were both amazed each time they took the correct turn, because the bulls had been through there only once before, and that had been a year ago.

Will and Dwayne starting bulls toward the breaks of Log Creek

Later in the morning, after Dwayne and I had gathered the bulls from the Vance Draw Pasture and headed for Thomason Meadows, the boys came out. Canon Ball brought Will and his horse out to where we had left our pickup and trailer. Will jumped his horse into our

On the breaks of Log Creek

trailer then drove it around to as near the head of Log Creek as he could get. He unloaded his horse and started back through the timber to where we were coming with the bulls. He knew the way because he helped his dad the year before. The three of us pushed the bulls on toward the breaks of Log Creek.

The mouth of the Corral Creek Basin is about eight or ten miles down the Imnaha from the mouth of the Fence Creek Basin. Out on top, these basins are separated by only one ridge. It forks down this ridge a short way. One fork of the ridge heads southeast and is the north boundary of the Fence Creek Basin. The other fork heads northeast and is the south boundary of the Corral Creek Basin.

Between these two forks of the ridge are Goat Basin, Falls Creek, Log Creek, Kettle Creek, and Pack Saddle—canyons that drain into the Imnaha. We headed down the ridge between the two big basins. When the ridge forked we kept to the north and went down a ridge that is on the north side of Log Creek.

Starting bulls down through the rims

As we made our way down the ridge we came to a place where a layer of rims that went along the hillside below us graded out onto the top of the ridge. The only way to get the bulls under this rim was for them to go down through a "chute" on a single-file trail. A chute is a narrow gap in the rim. Dwayne said that the previous year they had a terrible time getting the bulls started down through this gap.

When we got close to the chute we dismounted and tied our horses to some trees on the ridge top. We started putting pressure on the

Looking down Log Creek

bulls by throwing rocks at the lead to get them started down the chute. After some time of milling around, one old bull started down. It was slow going because it was so steep and the footing wasn't good, but once one had started, another one went, then another.

If a bull stopped part way down the chute we would pitch rocks at him to get him going again. It took some time and patience, but we did get them down through it.

Once they were under the rim they strung out along the trail and started on down the ridge like they knew they were going home. Dwayne chose this route to get the bulls down to the benches, so we wouldn't have to take them through the cattle in the Corral Creek Basin.

Will and Log Creek

Bulls made it down through rims

Bulls trailing down the ridge

The cattle were left in the breaks until in January when Dwayne opened the gates in the drift fence and let the cattle start working their way down to the benches. Since the drift fence, for the most part, was just across the canyon bottoms, some of the wise old cows had figured out how to grade down some of the ridges and hillsides and work their way to the canyon bottoms below the drift fence. Once they were below the drift fence there was nothing to keep them from going on down to the benches, so some of the cattle were already on the benches when Dwayne opened the drift fence gates.

When it started snowing out on top, it pushed the cattle down to lower country. The more cattle that went down on their own, the easier it was to do the gather. The winter of 2014-2015 was so mild that all of the cattle did not come down. There was very little snow, even on top at Buckhorn. Because it was so mild, the grass in the canyons was excellent.

Out on the points of some of the ridges there were small basins. Because of the rims and steepness of the terrain below the basins, they were accessible only from the top. One such basin was Brigham Basin, out on the end of Million Dollar Ridge. We could see part of this basin from Dwayne's cow camp, miles away up Horse Creek.

One of the hardest conditions to gather cattle in is fog. Dense fog can disorient a person so badly that he could get really "turned around" even in country he knew very well.

Dwayne had spotted a few cattle out in Brigham Basin so he and Will went in after them. While they were out on the ridge, a very dense fog rolled in. It was so dense they could not see the rims and gullies that were more than a hundred feet from them much less the next ridge over, or landmarks that would have helped them keep oriented.

Dwayne says he had never been so disoriented. They did finally get the cattle down out of there, but were unable to look around for more cattle.

As a last resort to find missing cattle in that rugged country, sometimes the ranchers will have a pilot, generally "Little Joe"—Joe Spence—fly them over their range. Jill McClaran, from the neighboring ranch had flown, because they were still missing some cattle. As they flew over the Corral Creek Basin, Jill spotted a couple of cows out on a ridge on Dwayne's range. Not knowing the names of the ridges on Dwayne's range, she tried to explain where the cattle were. From Jill's description Dwayne figured the cows must be on the ridge between Stubblefield and Dodson. Dwayne didn't want to get caught in the fog again so he waited for a clear day to go up after them. He had me come down to help him. We loaded our horses and trailered down Imnaha to the mouth of Corral Creek. We went just past the mouth of the canyon and parked at the Corral Creek Ranch.

Looking down on Corral Creek from Stubblefield Ridge

We rode up the bottom of Corral Creek, past the Corral Creek Benches, then up Corral Creek even farther, to the mouth of Stubblefield. As we proceeded up Stubblefield we once again were discussing the possibility of finding Uncle Billy's dug out. I took a picture of a cave that I thought might possibly be it, but later Jean Stubblefield Cook told me that Billy's hole was not a cave.

Looking across at School Flat from Stubblefield Ridge

We went on up Stubblefield, then graded back around the hillside, finally getting to the top of the ridge. We saw no fresh sign of cattle so worked our way on down the ridge, and still no cattle. We realized that if they had been there, they had left, but from the lack of "sign" we figured they probably had been on a different ridge.

While we were out on the end of the ridge, we started glassing across to Million Dollar Ridge. Dwayne retold the story of how he and Will had brought the cattle off of there in the fog. As we continued to glass we spotted two cows down in the rims. They were on a slope between two layers of rims.

Looking at three cows in rims across Dodson

There seemed to be a "seep" of water where they were standing. We continued to glass and spotted two bunches of elk up on the top of the ridge. We also spotted another cow on the same level as the first two cows, but upcountry about a half a mile. These cattle had probably been there when Dwayne and Will brought the cattle off in the fog—they simple couldn't see them.

Looking across the canyon, the cattle were probably a mile from us, but to get to them horseback, it would be miles. Dwayne said it was too late in the day to go after them. We would go the next day. We headed home, off the ridge the way we had come.

The next day we again trailered to Corral Creek, rode up it, but then went up Dodson instead of Stubblefield.

We went nearly to the top of Dodson then took a trail up the bottom of a little swale called "Mushroom." This swale was narrow, so there wasn't room to zigzag back and forth, thus the trail was quite steep. When we reached the top of the swale we started grading around the south hillside of Million Dollar Ridge.

Dwayne on Thunder at Pinnacle, up Dodson

As we went around the hillside we were constantly looking for the cattle below us. We spotted them, all three of them, but there was a new twist to the situation. The two cows had come back around toward the single cow, but they had graded up and were one layer of rims above the single cow.

We went on around to Brigham Basin. Dwayne wanted to make sure there were no more cattle there, and he wanted to glass the head of Thorn Creek to see if there were any cattle there.

Early morning glassing for cows in rims of Dodson

We couldn't find any more cattle so we headed back. When we got to where we were above the cattle, Dwayne dismounted, took his dogs and started hiking and sliding down through the rims. We had radios so we could keep in touch. I was concerned about Dwayne being able to get the cattle together. He would have to get the top cattle to slide down to the level of the single cow. I asked Dwayne to radio me when they were together.

Me on Duke in head of BC Basin. Background, Horse Creek

I started back the way we had come. I was riding, leading Dwayne's horse. I didn't hear from Dwayne for quite a while, then he said, "They aren't together, but at least they are all going the same way." That wasn't exactly what I had wanted to hear, but I kept going. When I got back to Mushroom and headed down it, Dwayne radioed again and said that the cows were all together.

Cattle we brought out of rims, going down Dodson

As we had gone up Dodson earlier that day we tried to figure out where the cattle would drop into Dodson when they graded back into the canyon. We figured it would be a little ways below the mouth of Mushroom. I waited at the mouth of Mushroom until Dwayne radioed to say where he was coming into Dodson, because I wanted to make sure I was up the canyon from him and the cattle. He finally radioed, and sure enough, they came into

Water Fall in Dodson

Buckhorn Lookout under horse's neck. Note lack of snow at the end of January.

the canyon right where we thought they would. I started down Dodson, met up with him, he mounted, and we started down the canyon with the cows.

The three cows were all heavy with calf. If they had calved up in the rims, the calves would have toppled over the rims before they learned to walk! It had taken two trips into that country to get those three cows, but it was worth it!

After a few weeks we moved the cattle to the east benches where they would stay for a couple of months while they calved. We took the mules and scattered salt along the middle benches and up under the rims above the main benches.

Cannon Ball saddling pack mules

Headed to the rims with salt

Horse Creek beyond Dwayne, Walking Cane to the right

Dwayne and I headed to the breaks to scatter salt

Taking salt to the high country

Dwayne would stay on Horse Creek, checking on the cattle regularly—watching for wolves. He and his dogs could do everything that needed done, until he started gathering to push them back onto the west benches—the first leg of the sixty-five-mile trek back to summer pasture. The grass was good, there was water in every draw, and the salt was scattered! The cattle were set for the rest of the winter and early spring.

Trails were frozen and slick.

Looking up Horse Creek

Ever since I can remember as a little girl being raised on Joseph Creek, there was always some "old-timer" who prided himself with being able to forecast the weather. Each of them seemed to take themselves quite seriously and was totally insulted if someone made even a slight joke about their "gift."

One old guy who lived up Crow Creek about ten or twelve miles from our place on Joseph Creek, really prided himself in his ability to forecast the weather. Occasionally he was quoted in our local paper, "The Chieftain." I can't remember his forecasts ever being more accurate than a toss of a coin would have given!

I tell this because some things never change. As the fall of 2014 approached, I heard all kinds of predictions, as happens every year, of what the fall and winter would bring. One of the most common forecasts was for a dry, cold winter. Well, they got it half right—it was dry, but it was probably the mildest, most of us can remember for nearly seventy years! Dwayne said, "If a cow can't make a living in the canyons this winter, she had better go to town!"

Spring Gathering and Moving Cattle 2015

Spring had come and it was time to start moving cattle again. Dwayne wanted us to ride the middle benches of the East Pasture and push cattle to the top. We both forded the river. I went up the Bull Trail and he went up the river/rim trail then up Washout Canyon.

We then moved the cattle to the Middle and Cold Camp Pastures. Dwayne figured we still needed to do some re-riding in the East Pasture and the School Flat Pasture. Some cattle were still along the middle benches so we trailered down Imnaha to a place where Dwayne could ford the river. He was riding Oscar (he hadn't become my Ozzie yet). He and the dogs crossed the river, rode up the river/rim trail then went up a trail to the top.

Dwayne fording river on Ozzie

While he was doing this, I took the pickup and trailer back to cow camp then rode out the benches to meet him. It had taken me so long to get back to cow camp that I expected Dwayne to be almost across the School Flat benches by the time I got up there. As I proceeded across the benches I became more concerned by the moment. The rim trail was pretty sketchy in places and he was riding Oscar who was a young, inexperienced horse. Once I had heard his radio "key." I wondered if he had tumbled into the river and as he fell it bumped his radio causing it to key. My mind raced with thoughts—none of them good—like how would I get emergency medical services contacted?

As I came to a high place I could see Oscar in the distance—about three-quarters of a mile away—standing on the brink of a gorge, and it seemed there were dogs around him. The quickest way for me to get to Dwayne was by following the road because of the gorges coming down from the rims. The road was very rough in places because of cattle walking on it when it

Dwayne on Ozzie, along the river trail

was muddy then drying in that rough state. Whenever possible I trotted or galloped Chip. As I got closer it looked like maybe Dwayne was lying at the horse's feet. Dwayne was wearing a bright red shirt that day so as I got closer I could see that it was indeed Dwayne lying there on the ground. My mind was racing—how would I get help; how badly was Dwayne hurt, and so on and so on!

How amazing it was that not only did the dogs stay with him, but Oscar did too! I went on the road through the last gorge then started up the ridge toward them. When Oscar saw me coming he started down toward me. I caught him and led him back up to where Dwayne was lying. I tied Oscar to my saddle horn then took a few steps toward Dwayne making sure I didn't drop my horse's reins; I was going to need these horses! I said, "Dwayne", but he didn't respond. In a louder tone I said, "Dwayne," but again there was no response. I then took ahold of his leg and gently shook it as I said his name again. This time he opened his eyes slightly, and groggily said, "Huh?"

"What happened?" I asked.

"Nothin'," was his reply.

"What do you mean, 'Nothin?' Then what's wrong?"

"Nothin' is wrong, nothing happened. I just thought this sunny, warm ridge was a good place to catch a little nap *while I waited for you.*"

My first emotion was relief then I laid into him! "Do you know you just scared ten years off my life!? Don't you ever do something like that again!" When I had settled down, we laughed about it, but I told him that he owed me BIG TIME! I still remind him of it occasionally.

Dwayne in rims on Ozzie

Looking down Imnaha River at Thorn Creek, from Bull Trail

When it was time to brand, the first job was to gather bunches of 130 to 150 pairs from the Middle Pasture and Cold Camp. The cattle were gathered and the first branding was done. A couple of weeks later it was time to gather for a second branding.

We gathered somewhere between one hundred and one hundred and thirty pairs and held them in the meadow below cow camp. Early the next morning we drove the cattle down Horse Creek, crossed the bridge then took them another half mile down Imnaha to a fenced meadow where they would be held for branding.

Jo looking down on Imnaha River and Corral Creek barn

Branding trap

Dave Kuhlman

Will, branding a calf

Luke Morgan

When we gathered for this second branding, the plan was to leave enough cattle for a third branding, which would be held a few weeks later, but we discovered a lot of cattle were missing. The east-bench pastures and the west-bench pastures are separated only by the Imnaha River. The flow of the river usually is high enough that cattle don't cross it with their baby calves. The spring of 2015 followed an extremely mild winter. There was very little snow in the high country, thus no "runoff" to make the river high. Because the river was so low some of the cows had taken their calves and forded the river, thus they were already on the west benches, mixed with the calves that had been branded. Also some of the cows that hadn't calved yet had crossed the river. There was no efficient way to gather and separate them, so these calves would have to be branded when we got them to Brushy.

Jill McClaran

Todd Nash and Dan Warnock

Todd Nash

Beth McClaran

On branding day, the "ropers" arrived. Pickups and trailers were brought into the pasture and parked in such a way that one end of the pasture was partitioned off into a small "trap" where the branding would take place. About half of the cows and calves were driven into this trap. The calves were then roped, stretched and branded. The cows were not separated from the calves; instead, the ropers went in among the cows and roped any unbranded calf. One roper would rope the calf by the head then another would rope the hind feet. The calf was brought closer to the fire where it was branded. It was then turned loose to join the herd again. When all the calves were branded, the entire bunch was turned out onto the hill so they could start grading up to the west benches. The second half of the herd was put in the trap and the process repeated then they were turned out to join the first bunch. The ropers were friends, neighbors, and other ranchers.

It was a common practice for the ranchers to help each other with the brandings. The ranches that have several hundred head of cattle have several brandings each year. It is not unusual for a roper to go to upward of a dozen brandings each spring, helping other ranchers get their cattle branded. By the end of the branding season in the spring/early summer of 2015, Dwayne had actually gone to twenty brandings where twenty-three hundred calves were roped and branded!

Snacks, water, pop, and beer were usually available during the branding. The workers—mainly the ground crew—didn't like to eat until the branding was completed because it was too hard to work after eating. The ropers traded off with the ground crew so everyone who wanted to rope got an opportunity to do so. After the completion of the branding, everyone was treated to a meal which was provided by the ranch whose calves were being branded, in this case, the 3V Ranch.

Maggie McClaran

Mark Dawson

Cannon Ball earmarking a calf

Chase Wallace and Erin Voss, Dwayne's daughter

Lunch is ready!

Dwayne on Crook; Luke Morgan castrating calf; Canon Ball assisting   Riley Warnock on horse; Todd Nash

The cattle were left on the west benches for a few weeks after the last branding then it was time to gather them and do "cleanup" riding on the east benches up Horse Creek, and in any place the cattle had strayed.

Dwayne picked me up at my place at six o'clock that morning, and we headed for the river. We left the paved road at the mouth of Fence Creek and started the slow, rough climb through the rims. We hadn't gone far when we came upon some cattle. One pair belonged to a neighboring ranch, but a couple of pairs, a bull and a late calver were 3V cattle. Bear hunters and fishermen must have left some gates open.

We stopped and I jumped my horse out, and got my dogs. I was to bring the cattle on to Horse Creek. Dwayne would go on and gather some other cattle. I sorted off the stray pair and started the rest down the road. The pair I had sorted off kept following us so finally I put my dogs on them. It spooked the baby calf so badly that it started running so fast that the cow could hardly keep up with it. The last I saw of them, they had crossed a bench and were headed for a canyon. At least I didn't have to fight them anymore!

When driving cattle in a pasture they are familiar with, they will most often take the best route, so it usually is best to let them pick the route, unless you know the area and know a better way. These cattle had strayed into an area they were unfamiliar with, and I had not driven cattle through this area before so I didn't know where the best trails were. My thinking was that since I was taking them back the direction they had come from, they would hopefully choose a good trail.

When the cattle got to the top of the switchbacks they left the rocky road and started around the hillside. This made sense to me so I let them go. As we proceeded around the hill it got steeper and steeper and we ended up above some rims. Finally, they came to a place where they got "rimmed in." It was so narrow they could not come back by me, and even if they could, they would have to go back about a quarter of a mile, at the least, before there was a place where they could slide down through the rims.

Bringing cattle through rims near The Switchbacks

I sat there a moment wondering what to do when the lead cow slid down through a solid rock chute that was about twelve feet long. At the bottom she regained her footing and continued on around the hill. Each of the cows then took their turn and slid down the chute. When I got to the chute I could see it was nothing I could ride down through. I wondered if I could even persuade Chip to lead down through it. I dismounted and studied the situation. There was a small pine tree at the top of the chute with its lowest limbs being just high enough for Chip to go under without the saddle horn hooking up. I ducked under the tree and had Chip come just far enough that I could go about three-quarters of the way down the chute before Chip started down. At this point there was a big rock off to the side of the chute. I planned to get behind this rock so Chip couldn't knock me off the rim as he came sliding down. When I got situated I gave a tug on Chip's lead rope and spoke to him. He started down the chute, bumping me slightly as he slid past me. He came to an awkward stop at the bottom of the chute, but was able to keep his feet under him. It had worked! I remounted and proceeded on around after the cows. We were now below the rims so I sent the dogs ahead and turned the cattle down to the road.

Chip, after having slid down through the rims

Another view of the rims where I brought the cattle and Chip through

The cattle stayed on the road and gave me no trouble until we got to Pack Saddle. For some reason, at this point the bull decided to "herd" the cattle. This is when a bull gets in front of the cows and won't let them pass him. He would push a cow over the bank and while he was doing this, the cows on the road would sneak past him. When he saw them going down the road he would run, get ahead of them and stop them. While he was doing this, the cow he had pushed over the bank would climb back onto the road and go on the road to where he had the other cattle stopped. Some of the cows he had stopped would climb the bank and proceed along the hillside. The bull would then run down the road to where he could get ahead of them. This would allow me to push the rest of the cattle down the road to where he would stop them again. This happened over and over. I thought I was never going to get to Horse Creek!

When I met up with Dwayne and told him of bringing the cows down through the chute, he said that as he was driving down through the switchbacks it had occurred to him that he had neglected to tell me to make sure I didn't let them go around above the switchbacks, but to make them come down the road through at least the first switchback. He had learned this the previous fall when some cattle went around above the switchbacks. They got into the rims and one cow rolled. He had learned the hard way, and so had I. After hearing his story, I was doubly thankful for getting out of there safely. Thank God for guardian angels! And I don't say that in jest.

It came time to gather Corral Creek and start the drive to Brushy via Vance. Dwayne asked me to be at his place at 6:00 a.m. I took my saddle and pads, but not Chip, as I was going to ride the little horse of Dwayne's—Oscar—that Dwayne had just agreed to sell to me.

We trailered to the head of Corral Creek and started gathering the cattle that had drifted to the top. Sharon and I rode the top, back toward Buckhorn. Dwayne, with Sherry and Duane Vanleuven, rode the south end of the pasture. We met at the "turn-out" gate with our cattle, opened the gate and headed for the Chesnimnus Cow Camp Pasture, which is on the way to Vance Draw. When I got to the Chesnimnus pasture I counted them through. We had three hundred fourteen cows, plus some bulls.

Looking across Cussin' Canyon and Five Point. Cattle are on point, three ridges away, and on point one ridge from me.

We had to stay with the cattle for three hours to get them to mother-up. We then loaded up and headed for the valley. It was raining hard when we got to the valley. Dwayne could tell that something was wrong with one of the hubs on the trailer so we went straight to Les Schwab and got it fixed.

The next morning, we headed for Corral Creek again. Today we would go down into Corral Creek and gather the rest of the cattle. Again it was Duane and Sherry, Sharon, me, and Dwayne. All of us headed down the Corral Creek trail. After going a ways, I took a trail that graded around into the high rims. There were cattle on every ridge and at different levels between Cussin' Canyon and Stubblefield. When I came to the north slope of Cussin' Canyon I got off and led Oscar because it was very steep; there was no good trail; and there was downed timber I had to get over or lead around.

The ridges between these canyons are made of a series of steep slopes, rims, and benches. When I reached the first ridge I glassed across the next two canyons to the ridges beyond. There were cattle on benches up and down each of the ridges. I could see it was going to be difficult to gather them because they were at many different levels on the ridges. These levels are separated by layers of rims, which in most places are impossible to get a horse through. The north slopes of the canyons don't have trails in most places, and have dense brush and timber. If there

They don't even know I'm after them!

was a game trail, it was likely covered with downed timber so a horse couldn't get through.

Knowing all of this, I radioed Dwayne and asked him, "What is the best way to get all of the cattle out of here?" He paused for a moment then said, "Well gosh, Julie, if it were easy, all we would have out here helping us would be a bunch of kids! Just work your way around the hillsides the best you can!"

I made it out onto the south hillside and was able to ride, though it was steep. As I proceeded on around through the next canyons I pushed cattle down to lower benches and trails. I continued to the breaks of Stubblefield then dropped down and started back.

Some cattle headed down Five Point so I had to follow them. It was rocky, brushy, and

Grading into upper Corral Creek

terrible. The brush ripped my slicker off the saddle while going through it. I didn't discover it until I was way down the canyon, so didn't go back for it. I had to lead Oscar through some places a horse should never be asked to go. When leading him through thick brush, he would put his head down to where his nose was almost touching the ground and wait until I was through then he would come plowing through the brush. He was so good! He never balked, but also stayed back far enough to not step on me. I had been impressed the first day I saw Cannon Ball ride Oscar, a few weeks earlier, and now I was even more impressed.

I got the cattle to the bottom of Corral Creek where I met up with Duane, Sherry, and Sharon, and we proceeded on up the canyon.

The drive to Brushy was uneventful other than the usual challenge of keeping the cattle that were in the pastures along the road from jumping in with our cattle. Dwayne had told Greg Willis that he would be coming through with cattle so Greg sent Klint Shaffer out to try to herd their yearling heifers away from the fence. I was up in our herd of cattle trying to keep them away from a weak spot in the fence when Klint came riding up through their pasture. He was pushing the heifers away from the fence, and doing a good job of it. We were both busy so didn't take time to chat, but did exchange greetings over the fence. Klint is one of those young men who you like from the first time you see him. I got to ride some with him later and it just confirmed that my first impression was accurate.

Each year this drive seemed to get easier as the old cows knew where they were going—all we had to do was have the gates open!

After the cattle were in Brushy a few weeks, it was time to gather and sort them for branding. Dry cows and late calvers were sorted one way, cows with calves that had already been branded another way, and calves that hadn't been branded were sorted off another way with their mothers.

Pushing cattle up Imnaha Highway. Dogs on both sides, working hard!

Little Horse is a canyon that is about half a mile up the highway from Brushy. There were 320 pairs with branded calves, so Dwayne wanted to push them up Little Horse. We started up the highway with them. Traffic always complicated things, though it was the fault of no one.

We finally got the cattle off the highway and started up the canyon. The cattle had been pushed up this canyon in previous years, but it didn't seem to help much. The canyon was quite steep. The cattle in the lead would get tired of climbing so would grade back out on the hillside on either side of the canyon. By the time we got the back end pushed up to where we could see what was going on, some cattle would be above some of the rims. The dogs were sent to bring them back, and were able to get it done most of the time.

Starting up Little Horse

There were places where the dogs tried to claw their way up through the rims, but were unable to do so and fell back down. There were other times when Will had to climb up on horseback—he was riding Drifter—to search for a way to get up through the rims.

We finally got the cattle to where Dwayne wanted them. We left Cannon Ball and Will to stay with them to see that they mothered up. Dwayne and I closed the gate and headed back down the canyon. We needed to do some more sorting.

When we completed the sorting, Dwayne and I went to the pickup. I took my horn bag off, threw it in the pickup cab, and was just getting ready to start unsaddling when Will came. We had left a pickup and trailer at the mouth of Little Horse for the guys. Will had hurried down the canyon, jumped Drifter into the trailer and drove back to the corrals at Brushy.

Will said a bunch of calves had gotten past them, scattered out all through the rims, and were headed to the bottom. Dwayne said, "Let's go!" I never thought to grab my horn bag, so left my camera behind. I missed some great pictures!

When we got to the mouth of Little Horse we could see Cannon Ball out on the point in the rims, trying to turn some calves back upcountry. Dwayne headed up through the rims to head off some more calves. He was able to use his dogs to head the calves down into the canyon bottom where Will and I were waiting. Dwayne's horse actually bumped some calves with his knees to get them off some rims! When that bunch of calves were in the bottom, Will and I started pushing them back up the canyon bottom. Dwayne headed back up through the rims to see if there were more calves.

Driving baby calves was not an easy thing! A couple of things helped us. This was the same route we took a few hours earlier so there was fresh scent, and maybe they even remembered some of it. Also we could hear cattle bawling very faintly way up the draw. The farther we went the easier it was to hear the cows. We got the calves through the gate, where some cows were waiting. Dwayne and Cannon Ball came with more calves, so we put the whole bunch together and started pushing them toward the top. We took them somewhat farther than we'd taken them the first time,

Will pushing cattle back into bottom of canyon

Dogs climbing up through rims

Cannon Ball pushing cattle through gate near top of Little Horse

to a small bench near the top. Most of the cows and calves were paired up so it wasn't long until we could leave. We all went back down the canyon and when we got down to the highway, there were four cows hanging along the road. They apparently had come down through the rims in the next draw over. So up the canyon we went, for the third time!

Dwayne had plenty of help for branding so didn't need me to help. I was getting a puppy from Mark Dawson. He was going to be at the branding and would bring the litter of puppies so I could pick one. I went down after church and they were finished branding by the time I got there. Carol insisted that I eat.

I visited with Mark about the puppies; he told me they were in a box in his trailer. A beautiful little male puppy caught my eye. He was the classic Australian Shepherd color—gray with small black spots—with a broad ring of white around his neck and up the center of his face. Mark had docked all of the puppies' tails. I told Mark, "That one is my pick!" The puppies weren't old enough to be weaned so I would go to Mark's later and pick him up.

Spike, my pick of the litter

When I went to get the puppy, I named him Spike. My hope was that he would be as "tough as nails" and a spike is the king of nails. Is that logic?!

I built a state-of-art dog house for him, which I named Spike's Mansion, and I partitioned off a part of the "dog run" so he would have his own pen.

After the calves were branded, the cattle were put in a pasture on the opposite side of Little Sheep Creek, across from Brushy. They were left there a couple of weeks then it was time to move them to The Divide.

It was June 13, so it was important to get an early start because it could get really hot in that country at that time of year.

I was up a little before 3:00 a.m. and on my way to Dwayne's by 4:00. Sharon met us there and we were on our way. We met Klint Shaffer and a friend of his, Joe Arnzen, at the mouth of Mile Post 17 Canyon. We rode almost to the top of Devil's Ridge then the guys went to the northeast; Sharon and I rode the southwest part of the pasture.

We came up this canyon in the shade. Note the Imnaha Highway far below.

Klint and Joe came to help because there were some Willis cattle in the pasture with Dwayne's cattle. These cattle needed to be cut back so we wouldn't take them to The Divide with Dwayne's cattle.

Lightning Creek Ranch from top of Devil's Ridge

Little Sheep Creek and Imnaha Highway

After the Willis cattle were cut back, we opened the gate and started south along Devil's Ridge. Cannon Ball and Will came down the ridge and met us. They had taken rigs to The Divide Pasture so we could load up and head home at the end of the day and wouldn't have to ride back down to Brushy. The drive was pretty uneventful until we got in the pasture where Todd Nash had his yearling heifers—lots of yearling heifers!

By this time, we were almost to the head of Devil's Gulch. It wasn't very deep or steep. Dwayne's cattle knew the way so they dropped into the head of the draw and headed for the gate into the Divide Pasture. We saw several bunches of heifers here and there on the little ridges. Some of the guys pushed some heifers out of the way then Dwayne sent Sharon and I on ahead to move more heifers out of the way. We gathered and pushed them north quite a ways. Sharon then went to open the gate into Dwayne's pasture. I took the heifers out of sight of our cattle and stayed with them a while.

Dwayne and Crook on breaks of Little Sheep Creek

After we got all of Dwayne's cattle in the pasture, we held them for the mothering-up process. We noticed a couple of Todd's heifers in the bunch. Each time the guys went to cut them out, they saw more of Todd's heifers. Apparently when our cows dropped into the draw, there had been a bunch of Todd's heifers we couldn't see. They just joined in with the lead cows and went along as if they knew what they were doing!

There ended up being quite a bit of sorting to do that day. We all worked really hard and the horses got a real workout. Everyone did his best but Will stole the show that day. He was riding Thunder, who could outrun any horse on the place. Others would be after a critter, trying to head it off, when Will, on Thunder, would come flying by, and get ahead of the critter. This happened time after time that day.

Will on Thunder, Dwayne on Crook

Will and Cannon Ball on Devil's Ridge, headed for The Divide

Putting cattle into The Divide Pasture

When Thunder came flying by me, I could feel the ground shake. His feet seemed to be pounding the earth. And even with this speed, he could turn on a dime. It was a sight to behold! It made me smile. Yes, the riders were tired, but the horses were exhausted by the time we called it a day. The cattle were settled for the summer, and this meant my riding for the 3V was finished until fall.

FALL AND WINTER
2015-2016

The summer slipped by and it was time to move the cattle back to Corral Creek to the fall/winter pasture. We gave Dwayne a bad time about how he could pick the very worst weather for the drive from Brushy to Buckhorn—he did it two years in a row—so on November 27th we started for Corral Creek and Buckhorn. When we gathered the breeding pasture at Brushy, the wind was blowing so hard we could hardly keep our hats on. The only thing that was in our favor was the fact that the wind was coming from the south—to our backs.

We made it to a Nature Conservancy pasture that first day. It had previously snowed about six inches, but the bunch grass was tall enough that the cattle were able to get some feed. It was a very wintery scene.

The next morning was cold. There were big divots in the snow everywhere the cattle had bedded. They seemed to feel better when they

At Thomason Meadows, headed for the Corral Creek Breaks

got warmed up as we started moving, but then the wind came up, stronger than the day before. I had traded my brimmed hat that I wore the day before for a billed cap with earflaps. I was wearing two pairs of gloves and pack boots that had felt liners. My feet still got cold, so I got off and walked the last four miles.

Dwayne had sent the boys after some hay because the Elephant Corral Pasture had no grass in it. The previous summer had been so dry that McClarans ran out of water in adjoining pastures. So they had to open the gates and let their cattle into the big pond in the Elephant Corral Pasture. Of course while the cows were there they had eaten the grass. No blame there—a rancher has to do what he has to do, and everyone understood.

Near the head of Stubblefield

By using both of the pickups the boys were still able to bring only about ten pounds of hay per cow, but it sure was better than nothing. It was the first hay most of the cows had seen since 2011. When we got out there the next morning there was not a blade of hay left!

One of the perks of the fall drive was that there was no mothering-up. The calves had been weaned long ago, and the cows had completely forgotten about them. When we dumped the cows into a pasture, we could shut the gate and ride off immediately.

Putting cattle down into Thorn Creek

The weather got progressively worse. By the third day, not only was the wind blowing but it was snowing. Again we were fortunate that the storm was coming from our backs. If it had been blowing into the cattle's faces, we couldn't have driven them, they simply would not have gone.

When we got to the head of Corral Creek we kept all of the cattle outside of Dwayne's pasture, except for a determined number that Dwayne wanted to push down a given ridge. At this point a gate would be opened and Dwayne would let a certain number through. They would be pushed down a ridge while the rest of the herd was driven farther to another gate where Dwayne would again let a determined number through. This happened several times until just the cattle he wanted pushed down Thorn Creek, Million Dollar Ridge, and the head of Dodson were left. After we put them through the gate the herd was split again, and Dwayne took a bunch out on a point in the head of Dodson. The rest of us started on with the remaining cattle.

Cattle on point overlooking Thorn Creek

Putting cattle down Million Dollar Ridge

Dwayne caught up with us and we split this bunch one final time. Dwayne took part of them to the south hillside of Thorn Creek; the rest of us started the remaining cattle down Million Dollar Ridge. It was a very snowy, wintery scene and by the looks of it, you would have thought we should have been gathering the cattle rather than putting them out to pasture. The cattle didn't seem to mind at all. They were in grass up to their bellies and there was lots of snow for moisture so they wouldn't have to look for water. They seemed as content as if they had just been turned into a field of alfalfa.

What a way to start the New Year! Just after Christmas, Dwayne called and wondered if I could help ride right after the first of the year. It had snowed more in the Corral Creek Breaks and he wanted to start pulling the cows out of the rims.

I knew it was going to be a tough job because of him needing help. If he could ride into a place and bring cattle out, he did it by himself, but if it was so bad that he couldn't do it all on horseback, then he needed someone to go in with him and bring his horse back out while he and the dogs went afoot after the cows.

Sunday, January 3rd
Elk, Wolves, and Cougars!

Dwayne came by and picked me up. I had a lot of gear: my clothes and my bedroll, my horse with all his tack, and my three dogs. This would be the first time Spike got to go. He wasn't quite eight months old.

Elk jumping fence between Maggie Beecher and Corral Springs Pastures

We headed for Horse Creek. It took us close to two-and-a-half hours to get there; it was slow going. We unloaded my gear and all of the provisions Dwayne had brought. Carol sent a bunch of delicious food.

Dwayne wanted to take the Gater up to the Corral Creek Benches and scope for cattle in the rims before it got dark. I jumped into some bibbed Carhartt pants and put on a warmer coat and hat, got some gloves, and we took off. When we got to the benches the first thing we saw was a set of wolf tracks. It looked like the wolf was just passing through. Then we saw cougar tracks—lots of tracks. It looked to be a mama cat and large kitten. There were cat tracks everywhere. Then we saw tracks that *really* got Dwayne's attention—huge cat tracks! It appeared to be the tracks of a big old tom.

Cattle in rims above Corral Creek Benches

After studying the tracks, we started seriously glassing the rims for cattle. What we found made our hearts sink. Cattle were scattered through the rims at various levels in worse places than they had ever been. Dwayne studied the situation for some time then concluded that he could not get all of the cattle out by himself. He said, "It's time to call in the troops!" This meant his son, Will. The cattle were so scattered, from near the top to not far above the bottom, that Dwayne knew that even with Will's help,

Cattle in rims out on the very end of Million Dollar Ridge

we wouldn't be able to get all of them in one day. We went back to cow camp and by Skyping he was able to make arrangements for the next day. Will was to meet us at the bridge at eight o'clock the next morning.

Monday, January 4th
Slippery Slopes!

We met Will as planned. He was to take the Gater and go on down Imnaha and see how many cattle were in the bottom. Dwayne drew a map of where he wanted Will to go when he got up to Dodson.

Dwayne and I rode up to the Corral Creek benches then up under the rims as far as we could go on horses. He got off, took the dogs with him, and started up through the rims. After he started climbing, I took his horse, Crook, and started up the bottom of Dodson, so I was gone before Will made it to the benches. When Will got to the benches he went up Dodson as far as he could on the Gater then started climbing up through the rims. We all had radios, so once Will got up in the rims, Dwayne told him where he needed to go.

Dwayne getting ready to climb up through the rims

As I went up the canyon I had to get off several times and clear debris that was across the trail before I could go on. I also stopped several times when I spotted cattle up in the rims. I radioed Dwayne to tell him what I saw. By using our radios, each of us knew where the others were and how they were getting along with the cattle they were trailing.

As I proceeded up the trail I came to a place where water had run down the trail and frozen, forming a large sheet of ice. One of my dogs, Jo, ran up on it then started sliding backwards. It scared her, so she dropped to her belly, but she just kept sliding until she was under Ozzie. As she slid under him, she looked up at me with a deer-in-the-headlights look in her eyes. I stopped Ozzie immediately so he would not step on her. Ozzie had on new "sharp shoes" and if he stepped on Jo it would have seriously injured her. Ozzie was able to walk right on the edge of the ice block where there were a few rocks sticking up, so he kept his footing.

Rims Dwayne had to climb up through

We had gone only about fifty feet farther, and around a corner, when there was another ice slide, worse than the first. It was steeper, with a bank above it and below it. The dogs went through the brush below the trail, but there was no place for Ozzie to go except right up the ice. I thought, "Well, this will really test these sharp shoes."

As we approached the ice, Ozzie cocked his head sidewise and looked at the ice, but he didn't refuse me. He stepped on the ice and went right up it. I was leading Crook. The horses

Cattle I spotted as I went up Dodson. Will brought them around.

did a little bit of slipping but made it through. When I got home I called my farrier, James Zollman, and told him how impressed I was with the shoes he had made.

I went on up the canyon to just beyond the drift fence and waited for Will to get there with his cattle. Will's cattle came into the canyon right at the drift fence. We let them drink then started them down the trail.

Dwayne had seen a baldy cow—black with white face—so he radioed Will and told him to go back around the trail he had just come on, and see if he could get the cow.

I told Will that while he was doing that, I was going to push these cattle down the trail past the icy spots. I knew they would never cross the ice unless they were being pushed. With me being horseback and having dogs with me, the cattle did cross the ice. There was no place for them to go but down the trail. Some of the cows actually had their hind feet slide completely under them and they slid down on their rumps.

Knowing that it is harder for horses to keep their footing going downhill than going up, I decided that even though I had made it up through safely, I had better lead down the ice. While I was riding, I

Cattle coming through rims. Dwayne took this photo from one level of rims above Will. Note Will standing on rocky point near bottom of photo.

could lead Crook by holding his lead rope, but when I walked and led Ozzie, I had to tie Crook to the horn on my saddle. Knowing I probably would have to do this, that morning I had put in some string to make a "break-away." A break-away is a weak piece of rope or string that will break quite easily. It is used in case one horse goes off the trail, the string will break before it pulls the other horse off too.

I got off, fixed the break-away then made my way around the ice by going up on the bank a little, where a horse could not go. I had a long lead rope so was able to get through the ice and situated in a safe spot then give a little tug on Ozzie's lead rope. As Ozzie made it down the slide, I moved forward with Ozzie so Crook would have room to come. Each horse slipped and slid but was able to catch himself at the bottom of the ice. We continued down the trail until all of the cows crossed the second icy spot.

With the cattle across the ice there was no reason for me to cross this second patch of ice. The trail was wide enough at this place that I could turn the horses around. I remounted and headed up the trail, crossing the top patch of ice once again.

I was beyond the drift fence a ways when Dwayne came on the radio and told me that his cattle had come into the bottom at Mushroom and he was coming down the trail with them. I found a place to get off the trail so as to not stop the cattle. As we started down the trail Dwayne radioed Will to see how he was doing with the baldy cow. Will was already back to the drift fence and waiting for us there.

As we went down the trail I told Dwayne about the ice on the trail. He was not at all surprised, as that strip of trail is notorious for having ice on it. In fact, Dwayne had packed de-icer on mules and stashed it in a cave nearby. When we got to the ice, Dwayne had Will go and see if there was any de-icer left. Many times the bears got into it, ripped open the bags, and scattered the contents everywhere. A huge pine tree had fallen across the front of the cave, but Will was able to get to the cave. There were three bags, so Will brought one over to the trail. They scattered half of the de-icer on the first icy slide and the other half on the second slide.

I didn't start down through the first ice until the guys had gone on and sprinkled the de-icer on the second slide. I wanted to give it as long as possible to start softening the surface of the ice before I rode down through it. It was amazing how quickly the de-icer made the ice soft and rough on the surface. The horses didn't slip at all.

We got down to where Will had left the Gater, and he took it and started home. Dwayne and I rode back to the rig, which was parked down on the Imnaha road. We loaded up and trailered back to cow camp. Will stayed the night so he could help the next day. We played a little poker after supper. Will whooped us!

Tuesday, January 5th
Not-so-sure Footing!

Dwayne rode Crook, I rode Ozzie, and Will rode Thunder. As usual, we parked at the Corral Creek Ranch and rode up Corral Creek to the benches where we again saw lots of cougar tracks. Again there seemed to be a mama, a large kitten, and a big tom.

When we reached the mouth of Dodson we stopped and glassed the high country, up where there was a substantial amount of snow. We had seen cattle in this snow the day before when we were glassing. Sure enough, they were still there, some out in the snow and some bedded down on a rocky point. In a couple of hours we would be up there.

We went up the bottom of Dodson to the Mushroom Rock. At this point we left the trail that goes up the canyon bottom and started up the face

Dwayne and Will looking at cattle in snow at upper right of photo

of the hill on a very steep zigzag trail. When we got quite high we started grading around toward where we had seen the cows in the snow.

Dwayne sent Will on to the top to see if there were any cattle up higher. Dwayne and I went on around. There were still a couple of cows out in the snow. They started on around the wrong way so Dwayne sent his dogs ahead. One of the cows came back my way; I headed her down to the cattle that were bedded on the point. The other cow headed straight for the top. Will radioed that he had found more cows on top. Dwayne followed the cow that had headed up to make sure she got with the ones Will had found, but she disappeared, so he assumed she had beat him to the top.

When Dwayne disappeared over the top, Ozzie thought we had been deserted, and he didn't like it. We were out on a hillside in the snow. Amazing as it may seem, the ground under the snow was not frozen. In fact it was so soft Ozzie's feet were sinking in six inches of mud under the snow with each step, and the hillside would break away under his feet. As he started jigging around, I realized I needed to do something to keep him busy so I rode back to a rocky point, the top of a rim just above where the cattle were bedded. At least the ground was solid there.

About this time Dwayne came back over the hill, so Ozzie settled down. Dwayne dropped down and started grading around to the bedded cows on the point. I planned to wait where I was until he got the cattle on the point started around the hill. As I waited, the cow that had disappeared over the top came back on the run and blew past me. It was a good thing that the trail was a little wider on the point of that rim. I followed her around; Dwayne brought his cattle around; and we met up with Will, who was bringing the cattle off the top.

The cattle we had spotted in the snow early that morning

Will, with cattle on the left. I am on the right.

We got all the cattle together then took them down the same zigzag trail we had come up. This required the cattle to change direction numerous times.

Dwayne had taken three female dogs that day—Becka, Allie, and Pearly. Each time the cattle needed to change direction, all Dwayne had to do was give a whistle or hand signal and those little dogs would turn the cattle. The hillside was so soft we had to walk and lead the horses.

We brought the cattle down Dodson to within a quarter of a mile of the mouth of the canyon. At this point there was a lone cow just above the first row of rims. Dwayne thought that maybe she would come down if we left some cows there in the bottom of the canyon. We rode back down to the rig, loaded up and trailered back to the Horse Creek Bridge. I jumped my horse out and started gathering the cattle that were hanging along the bottom. I started pushing them down the Imnaha Road while Dwayne took Will back up to cow camp where Will's rig was. Will needed to go back to the valley.

Dwayne brought the pickup and trailer and caught up with me down toward the mouth of Corral Creek. We pushed the cattle on downcountry to Thorn Creek, shut the gate behind them, and went back to cow camp.

Wednesday, January 6th
"Kind of bad in a few places"

I drove the Gater down to the Brown Cabin at the Horse Creek Bridge. Seth Tippett was building fence for Dwayne and he used the Gater to haul fencing material to the various locations. Seth used the Brown Cabin as his headquarters and occasionally stayed overnight there. After we dropped off the Gater we trailered on down the Imnaha to where we had dropped the cattle the night before. We pushed the cattle on down to the mouth of Tully Creek. I rode up Tully Creek and opened the gate in the drift fence so the cattle could work their way up to the benches and side hills where there was good grass.

We loaded the horses and trailered back to Corral Creek then unloaded and rode up to the Corral Creek Benches. New Year's Day, Dwayne had Little Joe Spence fly him over this part of the range so he could look for cattle. He had seen cattle up Stubblefield so that's where we headed. We again saw all kinds of cat tracks.

The plan was for both of us to go to the forks. I would take any cattle we found in the bottom down the canyon while Dwayne went to the top to get the cattle he had seen when he flew. When we got to the forks, we still had not found any cows so I was to wait there while Dwayne went to the top. He would then give me further instructions.

Dwayne got to the ridgetop then started down the ridge. He found no cows. He radioed that he was going to go on and lead off the end of the point and I might as well start on down the canyon. I went down the canyon a ways then stopped and waited. Pretty soon I saw Dwayne on the skyline. He then started leading Thunder off the ridge, heading for where I was.

We rode on down the bottom of Stubblefield. When we got near the mouth of Stubblefield, a couple of Dwayne's dogs that had been out ahead of us went crazy, barking and carrying on. They ran on even farther ahead of us. It was so timbered and brushy that we never could see what they were after. We figured it must have been a mountain lion.

When Dwayne was on top of Stubblefield he had glassed Dodson and saw there were actually three cows in the rims where we had seen one the day before—the cow we had left thinking she would come down to the cattle we left in the bottom of the canyon.

When we got down out of Stubblefield it was still early enough that Dwayne thought we might as well go after the three head he had just spotted from the top of Stubblefield.

As we were crossing the bench at the mouth of Dodson we saw where a huge cougar had laid in the snow. We could see the outline of his body, where he had laid his head, and even where his ear had been in the snow. Out behind this was the mark of a long tail. He was huge alright! No doubt a big tom.

We went on up Dodson to just below where Dwayne had seen the cattle when he was glassing from the top of Stubblefield. He dismounted and tied Thunder to a bush then he and his dogs started clawing their way up through the rims.

Dwayne and dogs climbing up through rims

The dogs really didn't want to go, so one or two of them slipped off and started back down. I saw them coming and radioed Dwayne to tell him that some dogs were coming back down. He whistled and hollered for them, and back up they went, only to slip away and start back down when Dwayne wasn't looking. I "tattled" on them again; Dwayne whistled and hollered again, and back up they went. This happened several times.

Dwayne kept climbing, but could find no cows. Finally, he hit a trail that had tracks on it. He followed it until he graded back into Dodson, at which time he realized it was the same trail Will had been on a couple of days before. It came onto the main trail right at the drift fence. He never did find cattle so he hiked back down the main trail to where I was waiting. It would take only about thirty feet of fence across the rim trail, right where it came back into the bottom of Dodson, to prevent cattle from grading around into those rims. Dwayne vowed that a fence would be built before next year.

When Dwayne got back down to me he said the rim trail was terrible. There were places where it was just two-and-a-half- to three-feet wide and went around cliffs that dropped off for 100 feet. At these places Dwayne dared not look over the edge for fear of getting dizzy. He had to keep his eyes on the trail!

No wonder Dwayne—looking at it from above, and I, looking at it from below—had thought there was no way in the world cattle could get around those rims. After Will had brought cattle around that trail a couple of days earlier, we asked him how it was. Will is a soft-spoken guy of few words. His response was, "Oh, it was kind of bad in a few places." Dwayne just shook his head.

I told Dwayne, "I just hate it when we get skunked!" to which he replied, "Well, sometimes it happens." He was such a cool head he didn't let it raise his blood pressure. That's probably part of the reason he could climb those hills as if he were only thirty years old!

Thursday, January 7th
A Bull, a Dog, and a Bluff!

We headed up the Imnaha road to Log Creek to get some cattle that had gotten into that drainage. Dwayne spotted them when he had flown over. There were four critters up high in Log Creek and one out on the Pack Saddle side of Log Creek. He had determined that the lone critter on the Pack Saddle side was a baldy bull.

When we had unloaded at the mouth of Log Creek, there was a rig parked there, and a hunter climbing the ridge, headed toward the four critters up on a little bench. When we got to the "dogleg" up Log Creek, where the canyon makes an "S" shaped curve, there were two more hunters.

We told them we were sorry and hoped we didn't wreck their hunt. They were really nice about it and said, "Things happen!" We went on up to just above the dogleg.

At this point Dwayne started to grade around back toward the four critters on the little bench. He told me to go on up the canyon a ways before I started grading back around on my side of the canyon. I had not gone far when I saw elk on both sides of the canyon up ahead of me. I radioed Dwayne and told him. He told me to start grading back around the hill so I wouldn't wreck the guys' hunt. As I went back around above the hunters I hollered down and told them about the elk. Later Dwayne told me he heard two shots from up that direction. I heard three shots from over on Dwayne's side. I could see elk in several locations.

Note cattle on ridge in mid upper part of photo

Dwayne and his horse are the little dot in the middle of this photo

I graded on out to the point, and sure enough, there was a bedding ground where a critter had been recently. I stayed there a while, giving Dwayne a chance to spot the bull on my side of the canyon, and radio me in case the bull was under a rim where I couldn't see him. It was cold, and the wind was blowing. I turned my back to the wind and kept looking up country, and around to the point that was above Pack Saddle. That point was about three-quarters of a mile away by trail.

After some time, on the very end of that far point, just above some rims, I saw a white face and some "black." I put my monocular on it and sure enough, it was the bull.

It was such rugged country, with no established trails, I knew I would have to walk and lead Thunder. I radioed Dwayne and told him that I had spotted the bull and was going after him. Dwayne could look across and see my location on the point. I wanted him to know exactly where I was in case he had to come to my rescue.

I dropped off the ridge and found a place where a few critters had walked sometime in the past. It hadn't been used enough to be beaten out to become a trail. As I went around the hillside I came upon the tracks of the bull as he had gone through the rims to get out to that point. I followed them around to the point the bull was on. When I was almost to the bull I pulled up on the point a little ways, to make sure I was above the bull. I then dropped in behind him so he wouldn't go the wrong way—onto the 'north' on the Pack Saddle side of the point.

I mounted Thunder and sat there for some time viewing the beauty of the Imnaha canyon, both upriver and downriver. I could see cattle on the flats down at Pack Saddle. I took some pictures and marveled at God's magnificent creation.

I figured it was going to be a "piece of cake" getting the bull to follow his own tracks back out of there. I started Thunder toward the bull, but he did not move. I got a little closer and instead of starting around the right way, the bull blew past me, heading for the north. I whirled Thunder around and was able to get ahead of the bull, but once again he blew past me and headed for the north. We were on a bluff that dropped off for probably a hundred feet.

Where the bull had bedded. I spotted him just above rims on point in upper left of photo.

Looking down on bull, and up the Imnaha Canyon

Close-up of bull

I radioed Dwayne and told him that I was having some trouble. He said he had been able to get the critters he was after and he was headed back to the dogleg. When he got there he would drop his critters and come my direction to help me.

The bull started around a little trail on the north that was frozen and had about an inch of snow on it. When I had last talked to Dwayne he said he knew which point I was talking about and I was absolutely not to go past it. I was, under no circumstances, to go onto that north, no matter what happened! I got off Thunder, tied him to a rock then walked out onto a rocky point where I could see what the bull was doing. In complete helplessness I watched the bull go around above a 100-foot bluff. He slipped with each step then came to a broken-down elderberry bush. As he crawled through it, I was sure he would go over the cliff. Just beyond, the trail widened then became so narrow that the bull could see he couldn't go on. He paused for a moment then turned around and looked at me. I figured that if I got away from there maybe he would come back out. This point had a little knob out at the very end of it. Uphill from that knob was a little saddle, or swale then above the swale the ridge was steep and rocky—the top of rocky bluffs in the north.

I got Thunder and led him up along the brink of the ridge until we were just above the saddle. I tied him to a rock again then I climbed on up the ridge a ways. I thought that if I could get to where I was behind the bull maybe I could roll rocks down behind him to encourage him to come out.

I was so intent on my climbing that I did not notice that Paige, one of my dogs, had slipped away. All of a sudden I heard the growling sound that dogs often make when they go after a critter. I heard the clatter of feet and rocks rolling and clattering as they went over the bluff and landed on the rocks below.

Bull heading around above rims

Trail Dwayne looked down from and told me not to go around it!

Looking down the Imnaha Canyon. Pack Saddle at bottom of photo

I instantly started screaming, "Get back here, dogs, get back here!" Then all was silent. I knew one of the dogs had caused the bull to go over the bluff! I looked around and saw that Jo and Spike were with me but Paige was gone. In a little while Paige came slinking up through the rocks with her tail between her legs. She knew she had done wrong and was in big trouble!

I crawled up to the edge of the cliff and looked over, trying to see if I could spot the body of the dead bull. I couldn't see him so I made my way back down the ridge a ways and looked over again. I still couldn't see the bull so went on down a little farther. I did this several more times before getting back down close to where I had left Thunder. My stomach was tied in knots knowing my dog had caused Dwayne to lose a bull. Those bulls weren't cheap!

I was being very careful not to trip, so paying attention to where I was putting my feet I wasn't looking beyond a few feet from me. When I was almost down to Thunder, I did stop and look up. There in the saddle just beyond Thunder was the bull! He had climbed up the slope to the saddle rather than go around the knob on the trail he had gone in on. The slope off that saddle was frozen, had an inch of snow on it, and was grassy. It had no rocks to give the bull footing. It was amazing that he had not slid down the slope and over the cliff. Another miracle!

Bringing critters down Log Creek

I slipped in behind him and tried to ease him toward the south slope, but he turned as to go back onto the north. I guess it was because he could see the cattle below on the benches at Pack Saddle that he was so determined to go that direction. At this place I could slip down through the rocks safely and get ahead of him, which I did. When he saw me he turned and headed around the south slope. I guess he finally figured he was whipped. He gave me no more trouble. In fact, he went so well that I couldn't keep up with him.

The bull chose a route just a little lower than the way I had gone in. I led Thunder all the way out and made it, fine. When we got back almost to the point where I had been when I first spotted the bull, the trail we were on went around a very narrow ledge. The bull was so far ahead of me that I didn't see what he did when he came to this place. I was following his tracks when Dwayne appeared on the ledge above me and said, "Don't go around that Julie, don't go around that!"

As I was coming to this bluff I thought it looked like something I couldn't get around so I was looking for places I could grade up around it. There was a place about a hundred feet back where I could grade out. Where I was when Dwayne called to me was wide enough that I could turn Thunder around and go back. As I stopped to evaluate the situation I saw the tracks of the bull going up through the rocks. It was a place Thunder could go up, but I couldn't lead without probably getting stepped on as Thunder scrambled up through the rocks. With Dwayne and Crook being above us I knew Thunder would stop when he got to them so I started him up through the rocks, gave the lead rope a flip so it flew up over the saddle, and let him go. After Thunder was to the top I crawled up through the rocks. Dwayne said the bull was going on around the hillside, headed for the critters he had left just above the dogleg.

Looking up at rims where the bull was trying to get away from me.

We mounted and graded around, back into the bottom of Log Creek. We got the bull with the other critters and went on down Log Creek without further incident.

When we got to the mouth of Log Creek I started down the road toward Pack Saddle with the critters. Dwayne loaded Crook and went on to gather some strays around Pack Saddle. This time Dwayne did remind me to take the cattle down around at least one switchback so they wouldn't end up above the rims like they had before! When I got to Pack Saddle we put all the cattle together then headed toward Horse Creek. We ran out of daylight so we dropped the critters and planned to pick them up the next morning.

Friday, January 8th
Crazy Larry!

We loaded up and trailered to where we had dropped the cattle the night before. I jumped my horse out and started these cattle on toward home while Dwayne took the rig back to where the Maggie Beecher Road takes off to go around the benches. We pushed my cattle on down the road then both of us went around toward the Maggie Beecher Pasture.

As we were picking up more and more cattle we were also picking up some bulls, which had gotten in with the cows. Dwayne wanted to separate them from the cows. There were cows just outside the Maggie Beecher Pasture and some in the pasture. The gate was open because Seth, the fence builder had left it open knowing that we were going to be riding there that morning. We wanted to push the cattle that were outside the pasture into the pasture then separate the bull and take him back to the bunch we had left on the road. When the bull saw us coming he headed for the gate. I galloped around the road trying to get ahead of him, but the faster I went, the faster the bull went.

The dogs usually are a lot of help, but there are times when they do just exactly the wrong thing, and you want to kill them! This was one of those times. I hadn't told them to "get around"—I hadn't told them to do anything—so while I was trying to get ahead of the bull, they were chasing him, making him go faster. He shot through the gate and I realized what my dogs were doing. I called them off and scolded them severely.

I was able to get ahead of the bull and by putting a cow with him, I took them back through the gate and we took them around to the cattle we had left on the road. We pushed all of them across the Horse Creek Bridge and started them up the Horse Creek Road.

Dwayne's horse, Crook, had thrown a shoe so he loaded him and said he was going to go to cow camp and trade horses—he would get Thunder. I continued on with the cattle. We had set all of the gates before we left so that we could drive the cattle through the meadow, past the cabin, and on into the corral.

The bulls looked really good, but Dwayne decided he wanted to put some Pour-On on the bulls before we pushed them on up Horse Creek the next day. He didn't have any Pour-On there at Horse Creek so he got on Skype and made arrangements for Carol to bring some, and his shoeing kit, to the Imnaha Store and he would pick them up later that night.

It had taken him so long to make all of these arrangements, and the cattle moved so well, that I was to the cabin by the time he got off the computer. He figured there was no need to switch horses at this point so he mounted Crook and we put the cattle in the corral.

It seems that every day on the 3V Ranch there is some form of excitement. This day had gone too smoothly thus far. Something must be in the wind!

As we had picked up strays all along the benches from Log Creek to Horse Creek, we picked up some McClaran cattle. Dwayne had been seeing these cattle as he traveled the road. He thought a McClaran bull that had been in his herd last year was back again. McClarans had accurately named this bull "Crazy Larry." When I saw the bull I wasn't sure it was Crazy Larry, but Dwayne was sure. Dwayne said, "We'll find out when we get him in the corral."

Well, now we had him in the corral. This bull was fine if handled horseback, unless he was cornered, but if you were afoot he would come after you immediately. Dwayne figured Crook would be fine in the corral even though he had thrown a shoe, because it wasn't rocky. He entered the corral on Crook, but because I was going to be the "gate man" I was afoot. I tied Ozzie outside the corral then went in. By the time I got in the corral, Dwayne had ridden to the far side. When Crazy Larry spotted me his head went up, he zeroed in on me, and fire was in his eyes! I yelled, "Dwayne, it IS Crazy Larry!" Dwayne moved the cattle around in the corral so some came between me and Crazy Larry. He was distracted for a bit and I was able to ease over to the gate of the holding pen that we were going to put the McClaran cattle in, so they could be loaded and hauled off.

I opened the gate and swung it way around. Dwayne separated Crazy Larry from the herd and started him toward the open gate. Even though the gate was opened very wide, Crazy Larry saw me on the other side of it and zeroed in on me. Instead of going into the pen he started down my side of the gate. I jumped up on the corral and the bull ran back into the herd. Dwayne separated him again and started him for the open gate again. I was still up on the corral. I figured I could jump down and close the gate after the bull went in, and that is just what I did.

There were also two McClaran cows in the bunch. Dwayne went to sort them and bring them to the gate. When he got close, I stepped over to open the gate. The bull saw me and came for me even though I was on the outside of the pen he was in.

The post that the gate was hung on was large. It was probably twelve to fourteen inches in diameter, whereas the poles on the corral weren't more than four inches in diameter. I knew that if the bull hit the poles he would break them, whereas I was sure he couldn't break the huge post.

I stood behind the post when Crazy Larry came at me. He poked his head around one side of the post, huffing and blowing snot. I slid over to the other side of the post and he came over. I slid back to the other side; he followed me still huffing and blowing. I could hear Dwayne yelling, "Stay behind that post Julie, stay behind that post!"

After a while Crazy Larry tired of the game and went to the other side of the pen where there was a Powder River panel rather than corral poles. He gave a huge jump in the air coming down on the panel. This broke the wires that were holding the panel in place. The panel toppled over, crashing to the ground, and Crazy Larry was out! Luckily, where he broke out put him right back into the bunch of cattle he had just been sorted from. Dwayne and I put the panel back up, repositioning it so hopefully it would be stronger, as it was braced against a corral post.

We decided to put McClaran's cows in the holding pen first, this time, so maybe Crazy Larry would be more content when we got him in there again. Dwayne cut out the two cows and we got them into the pen then he went for Crazy Larry.

When critters are really upset or mad and really want out, they actually lean on the corral as they walk along, testing for a weak spot.

One side of Dwayne's corral was made of small logs about a foot in diameter. Crazy Larry came along that side of the corral, testing it all the way. I had the gate open wide so Crazy Larry could see the cows, but instead, just before he got to the gate he gave another huge leap and landed on the top log of the corral. He broke the top log, toppled over, and was gone. He was now out with the cows I would gather in a little while, and take to the East Pasture.

We finished sorting without incident, putting Dwayne's cows out into the pasture where Crazy Larry had gone, and the bulls down in the meadow where they would stay for the night. Dwayne loaded the McClaran cows and hauled them to Cow Creek where he dumped them. He then drove to Imnaha to pick up the supplies Carol had brought down.

I'm trailing cattle to East Pasture

Meanwhile I gathered the Middle Pasture. As I was giving Ozzie a breather, my dogs started growling. I looked down and there in the tall grass was a newborn calf. I looked around and there wasn't a cow within a quarter of a mile, which was unusual; especially since I had three dogs with me. Usually the mama would spot the dogs and come running if the dogs got anywhere near her baby. I went on gathering the cattle then pushed them into the School Flat Pasture. I hadn't taken the cows more than one hundred yards past the gate when a cow stopped, looked back, and bawled. I rode up to her and sure enough, she had a messy tail and a big bag. I cut her back and put her back through the gate, which I had left open.

North end of East Pasture

Looking across at Corral Creek Basin

I picked up a bunch more cattle on School Flat. There were some really tiny babies in this bunch so as soon as I got through the fence between the School Flat Pasture and the East Pasture I shut the gate. With the gate shut, I could drop any pairs if the babies got too tired. I had put ninety cows into the East Pasture.

I kept pushing the cattle north along the benches of the East Pasture. After going around the heads of a couple of the big draws I started dropping the pairs that had tiny calves. I took the majority of the cows to the far end of the pasture. Some McClaran cattle were across the fence in their Lightning Creek pasture. I thought, "Boy, if Dwayne were here we could cut ol' Crazy Larry out and put him through the gate with the McClaran cows." I was still a quarter of a mile from the gate and it was getting late so I discarded that idea and headed home.

Ozzie had a gentle trot so we trotted whenever possible. Even at this, I ran out of daylight. When I got to the south end of the "short cut" trail, I lost the trail and ended up out on a rocky point. I rode down it a ways then came to a place that even in the sparse light I could see I shouldn't be riding. I got off and slid, more than walked, for a ways. It was one of those places where you were glad it was dark. If you saw it in the daylight it probably would scare you to death!

Looking across at Thorn Creek Basin. Buckhorn is on point in center of photo.

As I was going down this rocky slope, in the starlight, I could see the grassy slope on the other side of the draw. I saw a dark strip in the grass and assumed it was a trail. It was, and once I was on it, I was on the home stretch.

Elk were everywhere on the benches.

Dwayne got back to cow camp before I did and seeing I was not in yet he became concerned and radioed me, hoping I would have my radio on. I did, and I assured him I was fine and would be to cow camp in a little while.

When I got back to cow camp, Dwayne had put out feed and water for my dogs. I chained them in the barn and they each had their own feed and water pan. He had lit the lights in the barn so I could see to unsaddle my horse. He had supper ready, even fixed a salad. When he was at the Imnaha Store, Dwayne bought a head of lettuce from Sally. To be fair and give credit where credit is due, supper was pretty easy to fix because Carol always cooked up wonderful pots and pans of food for the main course and sent them to cow camp with Dwayne. All we had to do was heat it up and make a salad or fix some vegetables to go with it. When we came in tired after a long day it, was wonderful to not have to cook meat and peel potatoes. Carol used to send wonderful desserts and cookies, but Dwayne didn't eat sweets very often so that left them all for me, and I couldn't stay out of them if they were there. I didn't need them so I asked Carol to not send them.

While we are on the subject of food, Dwayne kept a sourdough jug going. He made as fine sourdough bread and biscuits as you could ever eat. Every breakfast, Dwayne fixed sourdough biscuits with gravy, fried eggs and some bacon or sausage. Carol sent wonderful homemade huckleberry jam. Because of these big breakfasts I never fixed a lunch, but it still was pretty hard to not gain weight when I was down there riding for Dwayne.

It dirtied more dishes to fix breakfast than supper so we left the supper dishes and I washed them all after breakfast. While I did the dishes Dwayne checked his "trap line." The last couple of winters the mice had moved into his pickup, both in the cab and under the hood, so each night he set traps, then the next morning he checked them. Each winter he caught about thirty mice. In the winter/spring of 2016 he caught over forty.

Saturday, January 9th
Tending the Bulls

The next morning, we gathered the bulls from the meadow and put them in the corral to put the Pour-On on them.

We sorted off four or five bulls and put them in the holding pen. Dwayne, with the jug and hose of the Pour-On slung over his shoulder, rode Thunder in amongst the bulls and squirted it onto their backs. We let them out into a holding pasture then brought four or five more in, doctored them then turned them out. We repeated this process until all the bulls were doctored.

We pushed the bulls up Horse Creek and put them across the creek onto the west benches. We had the dogs push them up and start them toward the upper end of the pasture.

The sky was clear; the sun was shining, and it was 33 degrees. I asked if there wasn't something more that needed done. I sure didn't want to leave the canyon! By using Skype, Carol had kept us informed of the weather out in the valley. It had been foggy and cold all week.

We loaded my gear and dogs. I was leaving Ozzie at Horse Creek because Dwayne had only Thunder and Crook down there to ride, and Crook had thrown a shoe. Dwayne was going to tack the shoe back on Crook, but he still could use a third horse.

It would be best for Ozzie if Dwayne rode him a couple of times a week until I got back down to ride. If I took him home, he would just stand around for two weeks and get soft. If Dwayne rode Ozzie a couple of times a week, he would stay toughened in.

On the way out we stopped at Eric and Jana Smith's, who live at the mouth of Camp Creek, to see if they wanted a puppy. Dwayne had just weaned a litter off of Allie and he was trying to get rid of them. He had already given one puppy to Tyler and Aspen Smith.

Putting bulls onto west benches of Horse Creek

As we came down the Camp Creek Road from Smith's, I said to Dwayne, "When you get down here to the highway, take a left!" He just laughed. That would have headed us back down the canyon instead of to the valley. He turned right and we headed for the valley. The farther we went the colder it got! By the time we dropped into the valley, off Sheep Creek Hill, it was foggy and 19 degrees!

January 27 through 30
Clean-up Riding

The bulls came off the west benches of Horse Creek, crossed the creek, wallowed through the fence, and ended up out in the Cold Camp Pasture. There was "clean-up" riding needed in most of the pastures. Dwayne had me come down and help with this riding. The weather was good and everything went without incident, which was unusual. After this riding the cattle were situated for the rest of the winter so Dwayne wouldn't need me for close to two months.

Cattle in rims near mouth of Corral Creek

Cows in rims of Thorn Creek. There are six cows in this photo...and three working dogs.

Imnaha River upstream from mouth of Horse Creek

SPRING 2016

Almost two months had passed when Dwayne called saying he needed help gathering and moving cattle. It was time to start getting the cattle gathered and divided into herds the right size for a branding. Some of the cattle that had been put east of the Imnaha River had crossed the river and were back on the benches on the west side—the Maggie Beecher and Corral Creek Pastures.

Dwayne came by and picked me up after church Sunday afternoon. He had the pickup and trailer with Thunder, Crook, and Ozzie. He had brought all of them to the valley to be reshod. The ground was thawed so the horses no longer needed the sharp shoes. The farrier, James Zollman, had put "toe-and-heel" shoes on them.

Jim Zacharias had put a picture on Facebook of the new ranch sign he erected at the mouth of Horse Creek, so it wasn't a surprise to me, but when we got to the Horse Creek Bridge we had to stop so I could examine the sign and "oooh and aaah!"

New 3V Ranch sign at Horse Creek   Photo by Sharon Gibson

I noticed that Dwayne had some lumber tied on the side of the horse trailer. When I asked him what it was for he just said, "Oh, we have a little project going." He kept a poker face and would tell me no more! From conversations we had had when I was down there in January, I had a clue as to what "the project" might be.

When we got to the silver gate I looked up through the meadow and sure enough, there was a new building. It was the bunkhouse that Dwayne had been hoping to get built. As some of the construction guys said, "It was not just a building; it was a piece of art!"

We kept checking the temperature in the root cellar. It remained at a constant 48 degrees. It was such a great place to store things that don't need to be refrigerated, but need to be kept cool.

In the winter of 2014-2015 Dwayne had gone down to an old cabin in the meadow and salvaged all the timbers and boards he felt were worth saving. Some would be used simply for decor and others for some of the structure. This little cabin had been built in the 1880s. It had been nicknamed "The Honeymoon Cabin" because Sam and Laura Loftus had spent their honeymoon there.

New bunkhouse at Horse Creek Cow Camp

Johnny Gibson brought his excavator down. A hole was dug, forms made, and concrete walls poured for a root cellar. The bunkhouse was then built over the root cellar, using much of the material Dwayne had salvaged from the Honeymoon Cabin. Johnny built rock retaining walls on the downhill side of the cellar/bunkhouse then filled in behind the walls with soil which he smoothed out so it could be sown with grass.

Monday we rode the School Flat Pasture and pushed the cattle upriver to the Cold Camp Pasture. The next day, Tuesday, our plan was to ride the East Pasture and along the river. We rode around the Bench Road through the School Flat Pasture and the East Pasture until we got to the ridge where the Bull Trail goes down to the Imnaha River. Dwayne would go to the bottom then down the River Trail and pick up some cattle he had seen when he drove the road a few days earlier. He would bring them back up the river, picking up more cattle along the way.

Looking up Horse Creek from Cold Camp

He planned to push the cattle up the Washout Trail, but some of the calves were so little he knew they couldn't make the climb. He left the cattle on a flat along the river and climbed back up to the Middle Benches then started south, picking up cattle along the way.

Meanwhile I rode to the north end of the East Pasture. There were cattle in the very north corner of the pasture—Crazy Larry was with them. As I started the cattle south, toward Horse Creek, I rode out around the breaks of each ridge. I was looking for cattle that might be just under the top—cattle that would be above the Middle

The red bull is Crazy Larry!

Benches that Dwayne was riding. After riding the breaks, I came back to the road, pushed my cattle along to beyond where the road cut through the head of the next canyon. I left the road and repeated the process. I continued doing this the full length of the East Pasture.

Pushing cows from Middle Pasture to Cold Camp. Note Dwayne and dogs up on flat.

When I was half way through the East Pasture, I had just come back to the road after having ridden out onto the breaks. I looked below the road and saw what I thought looked like a calf lying in the grass. I rode down to it to get a closer look—it was a calf. It was lying somewhat stretched out, not curled up, as a normal, healthy calf would lie.

As I looked at the calf I could see that it was breathing. I got off and lifted the calf, which was as limp as a rag. It is normal for a baby calf to be limp so that didn't surprise me, but it had some mucus in one nostril. I folded his legs under him and left him lying in a normal position. I remounted and started on my way.

After going some ways, up ahead I saw a cow coming back through my cows. She was bawling and obviously looking for a calf. I put my horse over the bank and went down the hill a ways under the road. I took my dogs with me thinking that if I was out of the way the cow would go back to the calf. As I waited I watched the road, but the cow never went back. When she got to the end of the cows I was driving she must have turned and gone with them. After some time I gave up and rode back up to the road.

I was pushing the cattle along when a big fall calf broke back and started the wrong way. When I kicked Ozzie into a gallop, he started crow hopping. It took me by surprise because I had been riding for several hours—it was not like we had just started and he was not "warmed up."

Pushing cattle into lower meadow at Cow Camp

Luckily it was a rocky place so he couldn't really turn it on, but he hit the ground hard enough that it caused my hat to go flying! He had been doing some silly things all morning, like whinnying for, and looking for the other horse. I had been dealing with this nonsense, knowing he just needed some riding, but this crow hopping, it was the last straw! If I had any pity for him having to climb the steep hills, it was gone!

I continued riding the East Pasture and pushed the cattle into the School Flat Pasture. Again I went out onto the breaks and looked down onto the Middle Benches. I could see there were no cattle on the benches below me. I knew there was a good trail up the Many Pine Canyon. It would be much easier for Dwayne to bring the cattle he had found on the Middle Benches up the Many Pine Trail rather than continue on around the benches. If his cattle came up Many Pine they would come right up to my cattle. I radioed Dwayne and he agreed it would be easier to come up the canyon.

My only concern was that I saw some cattle on a bench just ahead of Dwayne. If they stayed put, Dwayne would pick them up before he headed up the canyon, but as I watched they started moving. They must have seen or heard Dwayne coming behind them. Dwayne reached the top, hoping the cows I had seen were at the lead of his bunch.

I told Dwayne about the abandoned calf and the cow that seemed to want to go back. When we were going down the slope to put the cattle in the meadow at Cow Camp, the cow turned back and we let her go, but after some time here she came again on the run. She had a big calf with her. Not what we expected! She was still bawling and so was the calf. They obviously were not a pair. Apparently it was a calf we had missed and he was following us. When the cow met up with the calf she must have turned and followed him back. They both dove off into the herd.

We dumped the cattle into the meadow at Cow Camp. Dwayne said he would stay with the cattle until they got mothered up. He told me to go back and get the calf with the Gater. I gathered up a rope to use to drag the calf up onto the road with the Gater if I couldn't carry or drag him myself. When I got to where the calf was I realized the calf was farther below the road than I had remembered, but it wasn't as steep as I had remembered, either. There was a place on the point where I could get the Gater off the road. I drove around the hill to where the calf was lying. I was not able to get the Gater below the calf so it made lifting the calf into the back of the Gater a little more difficult, but the calf was little so I was able to get it done.

I made a halter-type contraption out of the rope and tied the calf so it couldn't get up. I was sure it wouldn't even try, but I wanted to play it safe. Dwayne heard me coming and started moving the cattle in the meadow toward the Horse Creek crossing.

I left the calf in the Gater and dashed to the barn to get my horse. Because of the rain, Horse Creek was on the rise. Dwayne figured it would continue to rise so the sooner we got the cattle across, the better. There were some small calves that would not be able to make it if the water got much higher.

Most of the cattle went across without incident, but there were a few at the back that didn't want to enter the water. I stood along the river edge and forced the calves that started down along the creek, into the water. Dwayne and the dogs were pushing them into the creek up river from me. If the cows went, the calves usually followed. One cow, who had a pretty big calf, would not get into the water so Dwayne finally roped her calf and drug it across the creek. Of course the cow followed.

We pushed the cattle up the draw that goes to Rye Bench. Again we stayed with them while they mothered up.

Cattle on Rye Bench. Note air strip

I have never seen it rain as hard on Horse Creek as it did those Sunday and Monday nights. The trails were getting more saturated and slippery by the day. The ground was so saturated that the trails would at times break away under the horse's feet.

We had the East Pasture Benches and the School Flat Benches clean, but there were still the cattle down along the river. On Wednesday Dwayne decided we would go in after them. He figured with there being two of us we would have a better chance of getting them out of there. Because the Imnaha River was running so high it was necessary that we go in from the top rather than down the road to ford the river.

We rode out across School Flat and into the East Pasture. When we came to Washout Canyon, we headed down it. Dwayne was in the lead. He usually didn't wait up for me or even look back to see how I was doing, but after we had gone through an especially bad "pucker place"—a place that might cause you to catch your breath—Dwayne went far enough to let me get through it too then stopped, looked back at me and said, "Some of these places were never made for the faint hearted!" We continued on.

When we got to the bottom of Washout there were cattle bedded on a little bench just above the Imnaha River. As we looked downriver we could see cattle on down the canyon so Dwayne went after them. I stayed and kept the cattle from heading up the trail along the Imnaha River.

When Dwayne got back we started looking over the cattle and saw there were two calves that had been born the night before. There was a cow with one of the calves, but the other calf was bawling and no cow seemed to claim it. With the dogs running around, a cow should have been claiming and protecting the calf.

When looking closely at the cattle there was only one cow with signs of having calved recently, the one mothering the newborn. We could come to only one conclusion: one cow had given birth to both of these calves. Both calves were licked off, so apparently the calf that was abandoned was the firstborn. The cow had cleaned him up then had the second calf and forgot about the first one. Since she was in the midst of a bunch of cows, perhaps that was what confused her.

So once again the cattle had changed our plans! The top priority was to get the "extra" calf back to cow camp. There was no way Dwayne could carry the calf in the saddle with him and go back up the trail we had come down. The only way out was to cross the river. We went to the river and started looking for the best place to cross. There was a place that, if he broke out some limbs Dwayne would be able to enter the river. On the other side, down river slightly, was a place Thunder and the dogs could get out.

I tied Ozzie to a tree and walked back up to where the calf was. Dwayne roped the calf then he had me run a front leg through the loop so the rope was around the neck and behind one front leg. He wanted a rope on the calf in case the calf thrashed around and went off the saddle, Dwayne could pull him to shore. With Dwayne pulling on the rope and me lifting from the ground, we were able to get the calf in the saddle in front of Dwayne.

Ready to ford the Imnaha River

As Dwayne entered the water he said, "I have to be sure I don't look at the water." If a person looks at the water it will make him very dizzy. When I was a kid, my dad would threaten me with my life if he caught me looking at anything other than the opposite bank!

As usual I had my camera with me. As Dwayne crossed I was praying for his safety and was thanking God that he was riding Thunder. That horse was phenomenal! He was a big stout horse that had energy beyond belief. He amazed me time after time. When I rode him, I knew I had a horse under me! He was Ozzie's sire, but Ozzie was not as big or as strong as Thunder.

The Imnaha was making such a roar that I couldn't hear Dwayne when he was on the other side, so we talked on our radios even though we weren't more that 150 feet apart. Though Dwayne made it across safely, there was no way he could ford to come back to me. It would mean that he would have had to ride upstream against the current, which would be asking too much of any horse, even a horse like Thunder, and there was no good place for his dogs to climb out on my side.

Dwayne on Thunder, carrying a calf that holds its head above the water so as not to drown!

Again, situations had changed our plans. The cattle would remain down along the river for some time longer. The new calf, the one the cow had claimed, would need a week or ten days to grow and get stronger before there would be any hope of getting him to climb to the top.

It seemed I had two options. I could ride back to the top on the trail we had come down, or I could ride the trail that went along the river and through the rims. I had ridden parts of the River/Rim Trail in the summer, but not all of it, and not when it was

Dwayne crossing Horse Creek Bridge. Taken from rim-river trail

muddy and slick. I finally decided to ride the River/Rim Trail. Dwayne tied the calf up so he couldn't wander and possibly fall into the river. He would go back after the calf in the Gater.

Dwayne never left me, but instead he rode on the Imnaha road and coached me as how to get through some tricky places. I would never have been able to find my way if Dwayne had not been there to say, "Okay, right in front of you, you need to switch back and go above that next rim; now you need to go down the slide right in front of you; now you need to drop into the bottom and make your way through the brush." We met near the Horse Creek Bridge where I was able to come off the hill and down to the Horse Creek Road.

When we got back to Cow Camp, Dwayne sent me up to gather the Rye Bench Pasture and push the cattle up Walking Cane then around to the benches on the west side of Horse Creek. I could see cattle on the slopes, on the Horse Creek side of the Rye Bench Pasture. My plan was to ride the hillside, pushing the cattle to the top as I went. The hill was very steep, the hill on which two bulls slid to their death a couple of springs earlier. As I proceeded around the hill I came upon the cow that had gone off and left the calf in the East Pasture. The hill was so steep that there was no way I could get ahead of her. I planned to let her grade around the hill until she came to the fence going down the top of the ridge then I would take her back up the fence to Rye Bench.

Riding Horse Creek Breaks in Rye Bench Pasture

As I was going along the hillside Dwayne came down Horse Creek with the Gater. He was headed down to pick up the calf he had hauled across the river. He could see the cow. I talked to him on the radio and told him which cow it was and that I wasn't sure which way she would go: back around the hillside, up the fence to Rye Bench, or dive off to the bottom of Horse Creek. Dwayne, in his undemanding way just said, "Just do what you can."

I got around her and started up the fence. Several times she tried to pull away from the fence and grade back around the hillside, but I was able to turn her back. After doing this several times she blew past me. I put the dogs on her and they turned her back, but then she refused to move. She was above a crossing of Horse Creek. I was in hopes she would go to the bottom and maybe Dwayne could get her if she crossed the creek and got on the road. I called the dogs off and sat there and hollered at her for a little while then sure enough, she headed for the bottom.

I went on to Rye Bench, gathered the cattle and pushed them up Walking Cane. Some cows crossed just above the fence and headed for the Horse Creek Benches, but others went quite a ways up Walking Cane before they crossed and headed for the benches. The cattle that crossed high up in Walking Cane ended up high on the benches—so high they had to come down a little ways to get through the rims. The cattle that crossed low, ended up on a low bench. I followed the high cattle on around the hillside. I could look down on the lower cattle, most of which had stopped on the bench. The point was quite steep so I dismounted and led Ozzie down to the lower bench then started pushing these cattle upcountry.

Dwayne had gotten back while I was doing this. He radioed me and said, "I have 'your' cow in the corral and the calf is sucking her." Sure enough, the cow had gone to the bottom where Dwayne had picked her up and taken her to the corral. He put the calf with her then put the dogs on them. This aroused the mothering instinct of the cow even though it wasn't her calf. She tried to protect the calf then let him suck!

When I was up on Rye Bench I looked across, and there were cattle on the lower benches of the School Flat Pasture. Apparently they were the cattle I'd seen the day before—the ones down on a bench ahead of Dwayne, that I hoped had come up the canyon ahead of him—but they'd come on around the benches instead. Thank goodness they had come most of the way. They would be easy to get. When I got back down to Cow Camp I told Dwayne about the cattle over on the School Flat Benches. It was early enough in the afternoon that I would have time to get them, so I brought them down and stuck them in the Middle pasture.

Up under rims of Grizzly Ridge, looking up Horse Creek

Looking down on Cow Camp from slopes of Grizzly Ridge

Looking across Horse Creek to School Flat Pasture

McClarans had invited Dwayne to a branding on Thursday. When we got up, the weather didn't look very promising, but the forecast said the weather was to improve as the day went on so he went to the branding.

Dwayne wanted me to do some re-riding of Tully Creek, the Thorn Creek Pasture, and the Corral Creek Pasture. When I had been over in the East Pasture a couple of days before, I saw one lone cow down in Tully Creek, so Dwayne dropped me off at the mouth of Tully creek as he went to Cow Creek to brand. The cow was gone from Tully Creek, but I picked up her tracks on the bench road. She was headed the right way—toward Thorn Creek. As I always do, I rode the breaks of each ridge and looked down on all the benches and into the draws.

The tracks I saw on the road disappeared as I got closer to Thorn Creek. As I was circling a point, riding the breaks, I spotted a lone cow in the bottom of a draw. It was so steep and rocky I had to get off and lead Ozzie. When I got to the bottom I remounted and rode toward the cow. Rather than move away from me, the cow turned on me, put her head in the air and refused to move. I made the dogs get back. I sat there for a few moments while hollering at the cow. Finally she started grading around the hill. I was hoping she would grade to the top, but instead she dove into the bottom of Thorn Creek where she again turned on me and refused to move. Sometimes cows move if a person is afoot and carrying a big stick so I thought I would try that. She did move, but dove off into the brush. The brush was so thick and low that I couldn't even lead Ozzie through it. Thorn Creek got its name honestly. This was one of those times when I had to admit I was whipped. I hated it when that happened!

I gathered thirteen pairs out of Thorn Creek and took them on into the Corral Creek Bench Pasture. Again I was riding the breaks when I saw seven head on a bench below me. I led off and started them up a draw toward the top. When I got near one cow I could see she had a newborn calf so I had to leave her. I took the rest of the cows and they joined the bunch I had brought out of Thorn Creek. I took all of them around the benches, crossed Corral Creek, and put them in the Maggie Beecher Pasture and closed the gate behind them. I had two calves that were probably not more than a couple of days old. They were exhausted from walking in the mud.

When I started that morning I had every intention of pushing cattle through the Maggie Beecher Pasture, down the point, and across the Horse Creek Bridge, but again the cattle had changed my plans. There was no way the tiny babies could go any farther. That morning Dwayne had said that if I got the cattle to the Maggie Beecher Pasture he would be happy. It was early afternoon so I sat for a moment trying to decide what to do. I could go on and push the cattle that were down on the Maggie Beecher Benches to the top, but if Dwayne didn't ride for a few days the cattle would just be back down in there and my work would have been for nothing.

As I had ridden the East Pasture a few days earlier I saw cattle on the benches just above the Corral Creek house (the Corral Creek Horse Pasture), but when I had ridden the breaks just an hour before, I could see ninety percent of the benches and there were no cattle on them, that I could see. Since I had not been able to see one hundred percent of the benches, I rode back to Corral Creek, went down it about halfway then took a grade road that goes around to the Corral Creek Horse Pasture. I figured that if I did find cattle, I would take them down to the river then up the road to the Horse Creek Bridge. I didn't find any cattle so I headed for Cow Camp, which was several miles away. I hadn't been at Cow Camp five minutes when Dwayne came driving in from the branding.

It was amazing what wet saddle blankets could do for a horse. I had ridden Ozzie four days straight and he completely quit looking for, or whinnying for the other horse. He had no "crow hopping" left in him!

We were planning to go to the valley that evening, so I had all my gear packed and ready to go. We turned our horses out. Dwayne fed them, the dogs, and the cow in the corral. We loaded my stuff, my dogs, and some things of Dwayne's, and headed for the valley.

It was 54 degrees at Cow Creek when Dwayne left the branding and it was 34 degrees in the valley when I got home. Brrrrr!

As branding time approached, it was important to gather up the "loose ends" and get the cattle all together. We had gotten the stragglers off the west benches and brought them over to the east side. Dwayne sent me on the Gater to the School Flat Pasture and the East Pasture to check "one more time" for cattle we had missed. Sure enough, I found three pairs in the north end of the School Flat Pasture. I went on into the East Pasture to look for more cattle, but found none. As I came back into the School Flat Pasture I closed the gate so the cattle I had found couldn't drift north into the East Pasture.

The next morning Dwayne sent me to get the three pair off School Flat. Much of School Flat used to be cultivated. Some of it is flat; some of it is gently rolling hills; but all of the cultivated land is virtually rock free. The "road" through School Flat winds out around the hills and back into the draws. Rather than ride the road that morning I decided to take a short cut up over one of the rolling hills. There were some elk bedded on a slope under the rims and above the "fields." As I got closer to them they got up and started moving around. Ozzie spotted them and kept his eye on them rather than pay attention to where he was going. As we approached the edge of the field, where it dropped off into a draw, I spotted the three pairs just under the crest of the hill. One of the cows was an "off-colored" cow, kind of a smoky color. Maybe that was what spooked Ozzie. When we were right on top of the cows Ozzie took his eyes off the elk and saw the cows. In a split second he whirled 180 degrees and a "run-away" was on! He tore back around the hill and I could not get him stopped. I reached down, grabbed the rein on the uphill side and turned him up the hill. We didn't go very far until he was glad to stop! I started him back toward where the cattle were. His head was high and he was as tight as a fiddle string. He just knew there was some creature that was about to get him!

When Ozzie had taken off it spooked the cows, so by the time I got back to where they were they had taken off in the wrong direction. We had to travel fast, but were able to get ahead of the cows and turn them back. Once Ozzie realized they were just cows, everything was fine.

There was a lone bull hanging around on the West Benches of Horse Creek just above Cow Camp. Dwayne sent me up to try to bring him in. I was able to get him back into Walking Cane, but then he brushed up. I went on foot into the brush and was able to get him out the other side then I went back for my horse. By the time I had led my horse through the brush and got out on the open hillside, I saw the bull headed up Walking Cane. The trail was up on the side of the hill a little ways, so I eased my horse in under the bull to keep him from bailing off into the brush again.

It was never wise to be downhill from a bull and I knew this, but if he got into the brush I knew I would never get him. I was in hopes he would pull uphill and maybe even turn around and start down-country. As I got right beside him he came at me! I quickly turned Ozzie downhill so the bull would not hit us broadside. He hit Ozzie in the rump and knocked us downhill to within a couple of feet of a bank. The bull dove off into the brush. The bull had won again!

I told Dwayne where the bull was, so that afternoon he went after the bull with some "bull tamer," which is birdshot in his pistol. He also took his .410-shotgun. While he went after the bull he had me and a couple of guys, Donny and Kevin McMillin, go up to Rye Bench and work on some fence that the bulls had torn out. We weren't far from Walking Cane, so we kept listening for the dogs to bark when they found the bull in the brush. After quite some time we heard the dogs then we heard gunshots. I had ridden Ozzie to the bench; the guys had gone in the Gater. After some time Dwayne radioed that the bull was coming our way and for me to open a certain gate, which I did. The bull went around the hill so high up that he missed the gate. I hurried on around and opened another gate.

At this point the bull was pretty well "tamed" so we were able to get him to the corral. We loaded him into the horse trailer because of his history of breaking out of pastures and corrals. If we got close to the trailer he would come at us and hit the side of the trailer. He didn't know it, but he was on his way to a "hamburger stand!"

The branding had been done; the cattle put on the west benches in the Maggie Beecher, the Corral Creek, and the Thorn Creek Pastures. It came time to once again push the cattle up into the Corral Creek Basin so they could start trailing to the top where we would gather them and start the move to Brushy. Dwayne had Cannon Ball picked me up Sunday afternoon, as he had already gone to Horse Creek.

After having gathered the majority of the cattle on Monday, we re-rode the following day. We found more cattle. Dwayne didn't feel confident that we had the benches clean. He knew there was the possibility that some cows or bulls might have broken the gate down and drifted back onto the benches, so we rode again on the third day.

Sure enough, there were a few cows back down on the benches. Dwayne and Cannon Ball started pushing the cattle up Corral Creek. I took a swing up into Dodson to see if there were any more cattle up there, since I had found some up there the previous day. I found nothing so started up Corral Creek to catch up with the guys. I was going up through a pasture that used to be a cultivated field, when I spotted a big heifer calf in the Sumac along the edge of the field. When she saw my dogs she spooked and headed around through the Sumac. I galloped down the field to the end of the Sumac to stop her. I radioed Dwayne and told him of the calf. He had Cannon Ball continue on with their cattle while he came back to help me.

While I was sitting at the edge of the Sumac, waiting for Dwayne, I looked down and saw the calf. She had left the Sumac, dropped down across the field to the fence, and was running down the fence toward the gate in the corner. I knew I would have to hurry if I was going to beat her to the gate. We were in a field on a hillside so it would mean galloping downhill, which would make for a rough ride. To make it worse Ozzie decided to do the "run-away" trick. He put his nose in the air and started running blindly. It seemed he would jump straight out into the air then his front end would fall to the ground, his front feet hitting the ground with a tremendous force. Each time he hit I seemed to loosen up more in the saddle. With the fence closing in on me on each side I didn't have room to turn him in a big circle. The ground was sod that had been eaten off and was moist because of all the recent rain. I was afraid to turn him sharply for fear of his feet going out from under him. It seemed my only option was to go out through the gate, down a bank that was about sixteen feet long, then onto an old logging-type road that ran along the creek. The bank and road were flanked on each side by trees and brush. As we shot down the bank and onto the road I grabbed leather to stay on—I was sure I was going off. When we hit the road I reached down and pulled him around enough that he had to run on the edge of the road, which slowed him down. I whirled him around and headed back for the gate to see where the calf had gone.

By my beating the calf to the gate, it had caused her to start up the hill along the fence toward another gate. I knew I couldn't beat her to this gate so I went back to the road, galloped around it to head her off if she crossed Dodson. I looked out over the open benches to see if she had beat me through the brush in Dodson. I could see nothing so I sat, watched and waited for Dwayne to get there with his dogs.

When Dwayne got in sight I radioed him and told him where I had last seen the calf. Even with a lot of searching, Dwayne and I could not find the calf. Dwayne finally decided that she must have beaten me through the brush and gone on around the benches. He said he would go on around and for me to go up and help Cannon Ball.

When Cannon Ball and I got the cattle to the drift fence and the gate we were to put them through, the gate was torn to bits. We radioed Dwayne. He said to fix the gate then for Cannon Ball and me to come back down to the benches and help look for the calf. Dwayne had come back from around the benches and was sitting up on a point where he could watch and listen for the calf. Cannon Ball went above the patch of Sumac where I had first seen the calf and I went below it. At the end of the Sumac there was a little hillside covered with all kinds of brush. I rode up along the bottom of it and there was the calf. I immediately radioed Dwayne and he came with the dogs.

The calf started up the canyon where we had taken the cows. We kept the calf in sight so she couldn't slip off and hide, but there was no problem. We got her up to the pasture and put her through the gate without any further challenge.

As we started for the rig I told Dwayne and Cannon Ball about Ozzie running away with me again. We had a three-way discussion of what kind of bit we need to put in his mouth. Of all the places I had ridden, with and for Dwayne, and all the things we had done, I had never been scared until this last run-away, but I have to admit, it scared me. I was sure I was going to get piled up and I knew it would not be fun!

It had been about a week since we put the last of the cattle up Corral Creek. Many of them had drifted to the top so it was time to start gathering and moving them to the Vance Draw Pasture. The first day we gathered about 275 cows plus calves, and nine bulls that were hanging along the fence on top. We pushed them to Vance.

The next day Dwayne was supposed to rope at a branding for Dan Probert at the Tippett corrals on the Zumwalt Road so he sent Cannon Ball, Will, me, Sharon, and Duane and Sherry to do the riding. Cannon Ball, Will, and I rode Stubblefield. Duane, Sherry, and Sharon rode the breaks without incident. As we went by the Tippett corrals on the way home, Dwayne was still roping.

We knew the third day was going to be a long one because from the top, we could see cattle that had breached the fence and were clear back down on the benches! The plan was to gather these cattle and push them to the top! All of us rode down the Corral Creek Trail to the benches. At this point we split up. Dwayne took Sharon with him and headed toward Thorn Creek. He sent Will up Dodson, telling him to go a ways beyond the drift fence, which would be a couple of miles. He had me take Duane and Sherry with me. We went toward Maggie Beecher. We passed quite a few cattle as we made our way to the Maggie Beecher gate.

Duane and Sherry Vanlueven and Sharon Gibson coming down Corral Creek

At this point I had Duane and Sherry wait until I called them on the radio. I went out the point overlooking lower Corral Creek then dropped down and went around the hillside, grading into the bottom of Corral Creek. There was a crossing and a gate there. The crossing was so brushed-in that I had to get off and lead Ozzie. I had to wade the creek, but I had done this a couple of times in the last two weeks so knew it could be done.

Cannon Ball and Will on Stubblefield Ridge. Dodson Basin in the background

I radioed Duane and Sherry and told them to start back to the benches, as I had found no cattle to send up the draw to them. I would meet them where the road they were on crossed Corral Creek.

After I waded Corral Creek and led Ozzie through the brush, I rode down the creek to a drift fence then turned around and started back up Corral Creek. I was searching the brush for cattle

Cattle in the head of Stubblefield

because I had heard some down in the brush as I came off the hill. I found them and pushed them up to the Bench Road. I waited there so I could keep any cattle Dwayne and Sharon would bring from heading down the canyon.

177

As I sat there, I could look up to the mouth of Dodson. The instant I saw him I knew something was wrong. Will was walking, leading Thunder. He was not really limping, but I knew something was wrong. He was about a quarter mile away when I first saw him. As he got closer I could see that his cap was missing. I didn't say anything until he reached me. I was on my horse so I looked down at him and asked, "Are you alright? What happened?"

In his soft-spoken way Will poured out the story.

Sherry, Sharon, Duane and Dwayne in Corral Creek

As he had gone up Dodson, the trail got more and more covered with all kinds of brush. Will had to duck his head and tuck his body each time Thunder plowed through the brush. He had gone through the drift fence gate and through more patches of brush. He had just gone through a patch of brush when he looked up and there was a big sow bear coming at him! The bear had seen him before he saw the bear. Thunder saw the bear at about the same time as Will so he whirled and tore back through the brush. Will had a radio hanging on a baler twine around his neck. He stayed on for a little while, but then a branch, or something caught the baler twine and yanked him off backwards over the rump of the horse. He hit the ground on the flat of his back. He didn't wait to see where the bear was—he headed down the trail where Thunder had disappeared. After he had gone about a mile he found Thunder stopped, eating grass. He caught Thunder and led him down to me.

When Will told Dwayne of the incident and he could obviously see Will was okay, Dwayne asked, "Did you go back and look for the radio and your hat?"

"No!"

To which Dwayne responded, "Well, if we didn't lose at least one radio each year, something would be wrong."

Oh, that Dwayne and his sense of humor!

We headed up Corral Creek with the cattle. It would be a long climb to the top. The cattle would have to climb up through the rocky trail that had been blasted out of the rims around the waterfalls. It was a cool overcast day, which made it easier on the cattle, horses, and dogs, but at its best, it still would be hours before we would reach the top. And reach the top, we did.

Heading up Corral Creek. The niche in the rims can be seen in the distance.

Headed for switchbacks, to top of 'waterfall rim'

Corral Creek Falls. Niche is at top of photo.

Being a very wet spring, it was wonderful for the grass, but it created some other complications. Brandings had to be scheduled around the weather and the trails were so wet in places that they broke away under the weight of our horses' feet. In steep country this could be very dangerous!

After we had the cattle gathered out of the canyons and moved to the top, we thought we were beyond dealing with consequences of all the rain. We soon found that not to be true! The cattle had been in the Vance Pasture for about ten days and it was time to move them to the Elephant Corrals.

The Vance Pasture is mostly a large meadow. It was not flat, but had a slight slope to it. It had rained so much that even with the slope to the meadow, the water was not drained from it. Each step of the horses' feet produced a squishing sound.

There was a place where the cattle had been salted. They had trampled out all of the grass and it had become a mud hole. The soil depth in the meadow was several feet, so the mud hole was also several feet deep.

Dwayne had bought some cows from a guy who wanted out of the "cow business." The cattle were a mismatched bunch that didn't fit in with Dwayne's herd of mostly Angus and Angus Hereford crosses, but the guy really needed to sell them and the price was right, so Dwayne bought them. A couple of the cows were horned and brindle in color—they looked like the offspring of someone's old milk cow!

Dwayne planned to sort some of the cows into the "cull" herd when we got to Brushy. Cull cows are ones that are old, or thin, or lame, or simply not raising a good calf. They would be separated from the herd and sold later that summer. The two old brindle cows were destined to end up in the cull herd.

When we were gathering the Vance Pasture, Will came to the "salt-lick mud hole" and found the two old brindle cows stuck in the mud. Will radioed Dwayne, who was riding a different part of the pasture. He came, and they put a rope around one of the cow's horns. Dwayne then tried to pull her out with his horse, but she was so mired down, it was impossible.

Cows mired in the mud hole

Cows after being pulled out with pickup

They were hungry!

Because we had trailered out to the pasture that morning, the pickup was not far away. We unhooked the pickup from the trailer and brought it down to the mud hole. Fortunately, there was a rise where the ground was dry enough that the pickup didn't get stuck. Each of the cows was pulled from the mud hole. They were partially paralyzed so could not get up or walk for a little while, but when they could, they each started eating ravenously! One had a baby calf which had stood by the mud hole waiting for its mother—the other had an older calf that had gone off to eat grass. All were happily reunited!

The cattle were moved to the meadows at the mouth of Brushy where they would be sorted into various groups for the summer. We had enough riders to sort cattle each way out of the middle meadow pasture. This required a lot of patience. Most of the time the riders worked slowly and quietly so as not to stir up the herd, but there were times when fast riding and quick turning were required. This demanded exertion on the part of the horses and riders, so by lunch time all of us were hot and ready for a break.

The Schwan's truck came back down the highway.

In the past when Dwayne and I went through the little town of Imnaha, if it was hot, Dwayne often stopped and bought me an ice cream bar. As we were sorting cattle this day, I got hot and said to Dwayne, "Where is the Imnaha store when I need it?"

"Oh, about fifteen miles on down the canyon," was his reply.

We hadn't sorted much longer when the Schwan's truck went down the canyon toward Imnaha. All in fun I yelled, "Stop him! Stop him!" We laughed and kept on sorting.

Heroes of the day!

At about noon, Carol brought hamburgers, fries, cookies and drinks. The burgers were the best I have ever eaten! They were so huge I couldn't eat all of mine.

After we finished our lunch and were about ready to go back to sorting, I looked up and here came the Schwan's truck back up the canyon. I screamed, "Here comes the ice cream truck again! Stop him!"

Quick as a wink Dwayne swooped off his big brimmed hat and started waving it. We all laughed and the truck sped on by.

"He didn't even hit his brakes," I said. "How rude!"

Again we were laughing and having a good time. In about three minutes we looked up to see the Schwan's truck coming back down the highway. He pulled over and started backing toward the gate that came into the meadow. Will ran and opened the gate—they backed in and two guys got out. We almost mobbed them! Carol had her purse and some money with her so she bought a carton of ice cream bars for us!

I dare say, it is not every day, when cattle are being worked, that the Schwan's truck shows up. What a fun, unexpected, refreshing treat! It just goes to show that you never know what will happen on a cattle ranch in the canyons!

CONCLUSION

"The canyons are calling me."
Julie Davis Kooch

I feel blessed beyond words, for the experiences I've had, and lived the life I've lived. The last fourteen years of riding for Tom and Dwayne have been the "icing on the cake!"

Being out in nature and viewing the wonders of God's creation never gets old. At the end of a long day, as we rode back to Cow Camp, we often found ourselves saying, "It just doesn't get any better than this!" There is a sense of fulfillment in knowing you've given it your best, even on those days when things went wrong and you didn't get done what you set out to do.

If God had not blessed me with good health, it wouldn't have been possible. How much longer I'll continue to ride for Tom and Dwayne remains to be seen. I do know I will ride as long as I have the health to do so, and as long as Tom and Dwayne will have me.

I am now seventy-one years old, but feel more like fifty-five. I jokingly say, "I have a new, young horse and a new puppy. I'm good for another ten years!" Only God knows.

As this book closes, I know the next time I ride for Tom or Dwayne, something will happen that would be "story worthy," but I have to draw it to a close sometime. Maybe from here on my stories will just be in the form of a journal. But whatever the future holds, one thing I know for sure—in my heart, I will always be riding the canyons!

Acknowledgements

"Much obliged!"

For borrowing the phrase, "In the Meantime, In-Between Time" (from the old song, "Ain't We Got Fun") for this book's Part One title, credit goes to lyric writers, Raymond B. Egan and Gus Kahn.

Again I thank Tom and Dwayne for making it possible for me to have the experiences I've had while working for them.

To Vernelle Judy, for connecting me with my very competent publishers.

To my publishers, Billie Judy and Jonathan Stratman, for helping me create this beautiful book. I'm so impressed with their perseverance through challenges, their patience with my limited understanding of electronic devices and software, for Jonathan's sense of design, and for Billie's 'eagle eye' in spotting errors in the manuscript. They were a pleasure to work with!

To Sharon Gibson, who persevered with me in our multiple attempts to get the cover photo. Oh, the hours we spent, the miles we drove, and the trails we rode to get just the right one!

Most of all, I thank God for giving me the life I've had, and for the health to do what I so passionately love doing—while keeping me safe during some of those "breathtaking" experiences!

"... never will I leave you, never will I forsake you." (Hebrews 13:5)

Made in the USA
San Bernardino, CA
27 July 2016